HANDBOOK FOR INVOLVING PARENTS IN EDUCATION

DORIS K. WILLIAMS

Humanics Limited

HUMANICS LIMITED
P.O. BOX 7447
ATLANTA, GEORGIA 30309

PRINTED IN THE UNITED STATES OF AMERICA

Cover Design by Ann Houston
Design/Typography by Daniel R. Bogdan

Library of Congress Cataloging in Publication Data

Williams, Doris K.,
    Handbook for Involving Parents in Education.

    Bibliography: p.
    1. Parenting— Study and teaching— United States.
2. Home and school— United States.   3. Domestic education
— United States.   4. Parents' advisory committees in
education— United States.   I. Title.
HQ755.7.W5   1985   649'.68   84-29712
ISBN 0-89334-084-7

Contents

Chapter 7   Parents of Special Children   133

Chapter 8   The "New School" Family Life Model   155

Acknowledgments

I wish to express my sincere appreciation to my parents, Ina and Dewey Keaton, and to my children, Bob, Ron, and Nan. Without them, my commitment to the concept of parents and education would not have been needed. They have provided me with an endless amount of inspiration and given both my personal and professional life meaning and purpose.

In addition, two very good friends who deserve recognition are Cynthia Seaman for professional editorial assistance and Chris Peper for preparation of the manuscript. Throughout the process they also demonstrated a great deal of patience and personal support.

Foreword

This is an impressively comprehensive book with much to offer all groups of persons committed to the importance of the parenting process. Those front-line field workers include parents themselves, who still have difficulty finding materials that are not either filled with jargon or overly simplified. Another important target group is the currently small but increasing number of students who wish to prepare for a career which facilitates effective parenting. And finally, the book will be extremely valuable to all those in universities who are called upon to prepare students for careers in this field and who have trouble finding textbooks that are both scholarly and readable.

Interest in the relationship between styles and patterns of parent behavior and developmental outcomes in their children is hardly recent. In fact, as traced by Dr. Williams in Chapter 2, it has a long and very distinguished history. However, there can be no question but that the "new wave" of interest has unique components which make much of the previous literature on the subject appear out of phase with contemporary family and social realities. For one thing, in earlier periods "work with parents" was somehow always assumed to be subordinate to "work with children." Departments of Child and Family Development (however labeled) generally tried to turn out students who could work directly with children without losing sight of family influences which could either facilitate or interfere with their work. Now, however, the emphasis is often subtly but significantly reversed— the parent influence is assumed to be paramount in the lives of children, with individual difference among children possibly influencing the outcomes that parental efforts can produce. "Parenting is Primary," proclaimed a conference that we held here in Little Rock a few years ago, and from this a Parent Center— not a Children's Center— emerged. With this shift in emphasis has come a genuine need for new materials concerned with the parental role in the education and development of children. This book provides an excellent overview and training manual which will be of value for years to come.

Having suggested that Dr. Williams' book will be of especial interest to three separate but related groups— students, parents, and trainers— I should like to go one step further and suggest that different parts of the book will be of special value to these diverse audiences. College students preparing for careers in the field of parenting will find the first four chapters particularly valuable, as they cover the history of parent education and provide an excellent overview of intervention models available for guiding local program efforts. Parents could not find a better introduction to the range of community support programs which can help them play their roles more effectively, nor could they find a better way to understand strategies for effective advocacy for normal and handicapped children. Those who provide training will find the full array of topics useful, but I should think they will be particularly excited by the last chapter, which allows them to dream and plan for a family life school model that more closely approximates an ideal educational program than those generally found in today's world. Certainly that is one responsibility of any author— to help the readers dream and plan and carry forward ideas which can be applied in their own domain of work. Such help is abundantly available in this volume, as the readers and users will quickly find.

Bettye M. Caldwell
Donaghey Professor of Education
University of Arkansas at Little Rock

Preface

This text is an overview of the concepts and trends emerging from the specialty of parent education. It includes definitions of topics, behavioral objectives, "theory into action" positions, and activities to encourage practical experiences accompanied by suggested resource information.

The material is designed for the student who is presently functioning in, or intends a career in, the parent involvement or family life field. This student will become the professional, who should have an assured competence and be able to translate theory into action. This student should also be trained to meet the expanding need for human services systems, for today professional graduates frequently accept positions in diverse organizations ranging from public schools and mental health institutions to related federally supported projects. The adequately prepared student will understand and be able to interpret the concepts of parent involvement and family life education. A learning tool such as this text will give stability and identification to the discipline and thereby help him or her achieve this goal.

My own parent education concepts began taking shape nearly twenty years ago when, as a mother of three young children, I had questions but no answers and quickly gravitated to the card catalog of the Ohio University library to get references on developmental behaviors of young children. Since then, my life-long career as a parent, a parent educator, and a teacher of parent and child development educators has demonstrated to me that what the profession needs is a reference book for academic instruction of parent education skills: awareness, development, and application. Principles of parent involvement in education vary considerably, but this book capitalizes on the emergent concepts of the contemporary social environment, the fundamental framework of:

The Parent As a Model,

The Parent As an Educator,

Education for Parenthood,

Parents and Volunteerism, Advisory and Policy Activities,
Parents of Children with Special Needs,
Parent and Community Support Systems, and
The Parent Education "New School" Model.

1. Introduction

Generalization

Parent involvement systems can differ significantly, with the structures and their components predominantly determined by the objectives of the organizations that create them. For instance, some parent involvement systems are really just infant education programs, while more traditional structures teach child development concepts to parents; then there are truly divergent parent involvement systems that are intended to enforce parent participation policies, like the structure initiated in the federally sponsored Project Head Start. Concomitantly, what parent involvement means to an individual of one system may be something quite different from the meaning derived by an individual of another system. Because the education of parents has such a notable effect on the quality of human development and family life, it is essential that professionals recognize the diversity in the field, know how the concepts have evolved, particularly in the last decade, and grasp the importance of the objective: to involve the parent in the education of the child.

Objectives

1. To review and identify the various concepts that make up the emerging field of parent education

2. To draw upon the historical antecedents as a way of providing the rationale for the field of parent education

3. To draw conclusions that will assist the professional student in understanding the "holistic" approach to parent education

4. To identify the professional role of Family Life Education

History

R.D. Hess (1980) traces the history of parent instruction to the early eighteenth century when agents in Massachusetts were appointed to oversee parents by direct intervention in the home. The goal was to establish the will of the parent as law so that the child would conform to parental authority. This was accomplished through direct confrontation and mastery over the child's will. Near the middle of the century the practice was relaxed somewhat, when less extreme tactics were used by parents to train their children in toilet habits, personal cleanliness, and exploration of the body. Emphasis was directed away from strict obedience, punishment, and the notion of the inherently evil nature of the child. Nevertheless, the father was still important in administering corporal punishment, while the mother was central to the internalization of moral values.

In 1901, a White House conference on the care of dependent children established a Children's Bureau, and in 1914 the group published the first contribution to the idea of parent education, the Infant Care Bulletin. Following this, many federal publications about parent education and family management were distributed. Yet, training continued to reinforce regularity and firmness until the 1940s when, according to Hess (1980), a dramatic change shifted the strategy from direct confrontation of the child to manipulation of the environment.

The Origin

The attempt to instruct parents in child rearing duties is not a recent educational innovation. Beard (1927) and Brim (1959) projected the traditional view that parents need to be educated about child development principles and, some twenty to fifty years later, White (1977) also shared this view. He believed that parents most need education about child development from the period of conception of the fetus to the child's third birthday. Obviously, the fundamental needs have remained fairly constant for nearly half a century. Perhaps a partial explanation for this is expressed by Brim (1959), Luckey (1977), and Hess (1980) who suggest that parent education did not emerge from a compelling body of scientific evidence or from stated needs of parents themselves. The theme seems to have developed from professional interpretations of human nature and from perception of human development concepts. Linked to social movements, this trend has given support to the rise and fall of ideologies and fads in professional thought.

The Total Approach

In referring to the total approach to Family Life Education Luckey (1977) describes it as a "'bastard offspring', obviously spawned of multiple parentage, none of which are eager to lay claim to it. . . further, the field is struggling to become real, to establish its own identity, and perhaps to declare its independence." Although Luckey questions whether the field of Family Life Education or parent education can be brought along from its "adolescence to productive adulthood," White (1980) seems confident that the educational climate of the future will foster programs to support the phenomena of parent education demands:

> ". . . it appears to me that we are going to see a steady growth of new programs to support new parents. We have witnessed a very dramatic turnaround with regard to the attitudes of people about child rearing. The best way to express it is to point out that, today, people who are about to have their first child feel no shame in saying, 'I would like to have some information about this job, and I would like to know where I can get the help I need in order to do the job well.' People were not comfortable saying anything like that until five or ten years ago. This change represents a radically different orientation toward raising young children than has been the prevailing point of view for many years."

Terms

Education for parenthood, parent effectiveness programs, parent-child programs, infant stimulation programs, family life centers, creative family living, and family living centers are all programs that imply some form of education for parents. An analysis of these programs would reveal concepts of communication and consumerism, as well as elements that would influence policy making and the dynamics of parent personalities, possibly to the extent of having an impact on children's socialization. These programs also indicate that academicians as well as professionals in the human service disciplines have a keen interest in parents' involvement in the education of their children. All too often, parent involvement is considered to be synonymous with parenting or education for child rearing. Admittedly, being educated to raise a child is important, but it is only one of the components vital to contemporary parent education programs or to a curriculum offered to the person who is training for a career in the creation and management of programs for parents.

In all probability, the term "parent" will remain a noun, but if it were ever to be conjugated as the transitive verb "parenting," then the titles of the chapters of this book, listed below, would undoubtedly be included in its definition. In the interim, the classification of chapter titles, analogous terms, and explanations may be useful in correlating the meanings of terms the reader knows with the meanings of terms the author has chosen to describe respective chapters in the parents and education manuscript. See Figure 1 below for such a classification.

Figure 1

CHAPTER TITLES	OTHER POPULAR TERMS	EXPLANATIONS
The Parent As a Model	Modeling, Socialization, Role Identification	Conscious or unconscious behavior of parent that sets examples and expectations for child
Education for Parenthood	Parenting, Parent Education, Parent-Child Interaction	Assimilation of information and practice of skills that will improve child rearing and enhance communication
The Parent As an Educator	Infant Stimulation, Home Learning Instruction	Educating parents to teach own children through formal techniques of scholastic stimulation; teaching parents to be child's first, most important teacher
Community Systems for Parent Involvement	Child Abuse Clinics, Toy and Safety Education, Participation	Exposing parents to community resource parent programs and the support functions of these programs; increasing parents' conscious awareness
Parents and Policy Involvement	Volunteer Staff, School Advisory Committees, Policy Development Programs	Encouraging and assisting parents to be active and responsible for the management of their environment, particularly in community and school programs that influence development
Parents of Children with Special Needs	Child With a Learning Delay, Child Who Is Disadvantaged, The Gifted Child	Identifying strategies that help parents understand and share in the care and education of children with special needs

General Definition

The distinguishing characteristic of this book is the assumption that parents and education are one with parents and involvement. Each writer bases his work on assumptions unique to his personal philosophy as an academician, social servant, psychologist, etc. Earhart (1980) defines parent education as a combination of all activities and experiences that provide information and guidelines for parent role. Morrison (1978) assumes that parent involvement is the inclusion of parents in classroom and early childhood center activities. Brim (1929) refers to it as a "conscious awareness," and Morrison (1978) further calls it the ultimate expression of education and development. Parent education and involvement for many people signifies the detached teaching of parents through group sessions, seminars, and lectures. Whatever the assumption, the objective of the professional in parent education is to understand all forms of involvement systems and be capable of analyzing their structures and interpreting the components. This can be accomplished only by having a concise comprehension of the goals of parent education.

The Parent As the Change Agent

According to Keniston (1979), most parents want to be self-sufficient and take the best possible care of their children. Society has held parents responsible for raising children without needed resources and influence, but as knowledge of child development increases, its use in parent-oriented programs is accelerated. The current interest of federal agencies in "strengthening the family" and in sponsoring parent education programs for public television will not dissipate, especially if the divorce rate continues to be high (Hess, 1980). Children are the only future we will ever have, and if we wish to keep the children of this future, the best thing we can do is to improve the lives of their parents. Brim (1959) emphasizes this distinction by saying that the evaluation of parent education programs should be dependent upon the behavior changes in the children of parents who have received specialized training for child rearing.

Literature Review

New interest in the continuity of education has recently been generated because of findings related to parents who are involved in their child's education. Since parents provide so many aspects of the child's total socialization and early education environment, it is reasonable to expect that any improvement in the parent will influence the child in a positive way. As White (1977) explains, his interest in the process of parent education is "how well-put-together people get to be that way."

Parents and Public Schools

The State Department of Education of New York, Division of Research, found in a 1979 study that the extent to which parents involve themselves in their children's educational programs affects the children's cognitive development. Parent involvement in this experimental pre-kindergarten program included school visits, home visits by school personnel, parent meetings, employment of parents in the program, and incidental contacts such as telephone calls.

Guttman (1978) believes that "parental involvement" or "citizen participation" in public schools is here to stay. There is strong support for the principle of citizen participation, but the concern is whether or not the idea can be translated into workable programs and studies that will have an impact on instruction. Educators who want parent involvement to flourish are looking for ways to collaborate with parents in developing the best possible conditions for educating children because reinforcement from the parents is critical to the success of the education. While institutions such as those described by Pierson, et al. (1974) in Brookline, Massachusetts, are concerned with optimal chances in school and in later life, there appear to be many non-cognitive, child-related benefits. For example, Nebgen (1979) sees a direct link between parent involvement in the schools and increased parent self-esteem and feelings of control.

Parent Competencies

Behavioral scientists have built increasing evidence that parents' emotions and personalities, as well as their relationships with one another, had significant effects on their child's development and the events that influence the youngster's life. Reports at an American Psychiatric Association meeting pointed to definite links between depressed mothers and the cognitive and emotional capabilities of their children, certain family types and the occurrence of father-daughter incest, and "super-rich" parents and the effects of their wealth and their life styles upon their youngsters.

Good parent education can improve the so-called "bad" parent. Society's goal should be to help parents live up to their roles and accept the responsibilities of understanding children from the unborn through the infant stages of life. Parents must know all the ages and stages of childhood and recognize the infant's behavior as a dependency, not as selfishness; further, parents should understand that the quickest road to the child's independence is by way of the parents' dedication to his psychological and physical needs during the dependent years.

Involvement

Parents need to be involved in their children's education to provide consistency between school and home. This can be accomplished if parents have been taught to provide therapy, behavior management, testing, reading skills, etc. As parents know more about educational procedures and techniques, they can be more active in the process of education (Kroth, 1978).

Suchara (1977) recommends six important goals for adults, particularly adult parents:

1. to lead children to value a world of diversity
2. to clarify parental values and philosophies
3. to become involved in decision-making
4. to model and foster positive self-images and caring relationships
5. to advocate for children
6. to work for greater coordination of services

Whether people want to be parents and are capable of being good parents depends, according to Keniston (1979), not only on their own psychological make-up but also on what society is doing to and for parents and on the cultural messages concerning the value of parenthood.

Model Programs

Magdid, et al. (1979) describes a 1972 Philadelphia program that was initiated because of an increase in teen-aged pregnancies. Federal funds under Title IV-A of the Social Security Act were obtained by the Philadelphia School District to support the Comprehensive Services for School-Age Parents program goals:

1. to provide social services
2. to improve health care
3. to encourage completion of high school
4. to improve the parenting skills

Nationally, Project Head Start, a federally funded child development program for low income parents and children, is possibly the most direct and specific system of parent involvement in the development, conduct, and overall administration of a program of education, health, nutrition, and social service. Head Start policy is predicated on the concept that the program's success demands the fullest involvement of parents or parental substitutes of enrollees. To meet this goal, the Head Start Manual of Policies and Instructions sets forth the following opportunities for parent participation:

1. involving parents in decision-making for program planning and operation
2. using parents in the classroom as paid employees, volunteers, or observers
3. providing support activities which parents have helped develop
4. providing opportunities, primarily through home visits by teachers, for parents to work with their own children in cooperation with Head Start staff.

Some consider programs successful if mother-child interaction increased; mothers were more understanding of child behavior; and children improved physically, mentally, emotionally, and socially. But Bronfenbrenner's (1974) research infers that early teacher-parent interaction is most effective and long-lasting when focused on the mother-child interactions.

Stevens (1978) admits that more research is needed but suggests that, in relation to parent-infant programs, effective systems are prescriptive as well as personalized. His narrative emphasizes a significant effect in areas of material teaching style and attitude, children's intelligence, language development, and exploratory behavior.

Another study by Endres and Evans (1968) concentrated on the effects of a parent education program on knowledge, attitudes, overt behavior of parents, and the children's self-concepts. But one of the most recent and challenging essays on the importance of parent education as validated by empirical research is the work edited by Fantini and Cardenas (1980). In this text, Hess (1980) suggests that much of the research literature cannot be generalized to family settings since relationships are not perfect and research relates to the scientific audience which is not a useful vehicle for prescribing remedial strategies.

Effectiveness

Hess (1980) reviews the effectiveness of parent education programs and does not give much basis for optimism when he states, "It is an extraordinarily difficult task to change parent behavior; some information, particularly that having to do with such discrete matters as safety and nutrition, is relatively easy to transmit to parents but not readily translated into action." Recognizing barriers of the most formidable sort, Hess says it must be realized that parent education is not education in the usual sense, but rather it is an attempt to change established patterns in the experience of family members. Hess (1980) rounds out the discussion by saying that our culture has now entered an era of concern for social effectiveness, mental health, individual fulfillment, and self-expression — all accomplished through the "human relations technology" of persuasive and behavioral manipulation of the child toward rational choice.

In a *Forecast for Home Economics* feature article, Brown (1975) describes an innovative federally supported model, Education of Parenthood, that combines the efforts of the Office of Education, the Office of Child Development, and the National Institute of Mental Health. An ambitious program, Education of Parenthood promotes and persuades schools and voluntary organizations to establish parenthood education programs for all secondary school youth, focusing activities and resources on four target areas:

1. *curriculum development* to provide programs and materials with relevance and universality
2. *technical assistance* in evaluating existing materials and in "linking up" outstanding programs in regional cooperative activities
3. *non-school based parenthood education* support by providing funds to community groups who are developing parenthood education projects
4. *public and professional education* to alert, inform, and encourage parenthood education

Because so much is happening under this Education for Parenthood banner, it is difficult to distinguish common activities that tie all these organizations together in the name of parent education.

In view of federally sponsored projects, there must be underlying factors basic to each Education for Parenthood effort, as follow:

1. comprehensive
2. competency based
3. interdisciplinary
4. experiential based
5. flexible
6. universal in appeal

7. equitable
8. cost effective

Summary

As far back as 1959, Brim suggested that professionals responsible for teaching and managing parent education programs could be individuals trained in a specific family life academic major, clinical psychiatrists, psychologists, social workers, home economists, teachers, allied medical personnel, nurses, clergymen, religious educators, and other parents. The list of potential educators has become anything but shorter since it was drafted, and the range has expanded over the last thirty years as the groups have welcomed, with differing tempo and intensity of interest, education and parents as part of their responsibilities.

Today the parent educator may be an expert in one or more fields pertinent to parents and education, but he does not consider himself a scientific technician who can furnish specific formulae for the solution of parents' problems. The "expertness" exists, rather, when educators help parents incorporate into their thinking and actions some of the attitudes and practices that may well apply to their situations. In some sense, the parent educator is a "middle man," who has a broad understanding of the elements that contribute to family welfare, such as nutrition, economics and finance, child growth and development patterns, social and community concerns, psychological variables, extended family member influences, and self-concept. The effective parent educator respects and recognizes research conducted by colleagues and expects to be able to augment growth in the parent at both the "feeling level" and the "intellectual level."

While parent education is not a panacea, it is the beginning of an attempt to meet a practical problem in both the preventive and the remedial sense. An analogy in medicine suggests that our focus has slowly shifted from diagnosis and treatment of acute and chronic ills to a growing concern for preventive health care which will reduce the need for medical treatment. In the field of mental health, we are beginning to examine ways to foster healthy personalities and thus reduce the need for psychotherapy.

Professionals recognize that there are no prescriptive answers to problems that face parents. As Hess (1980) put it,

"The new technology of child management focuses upon what a
parent should do in particular situations, or the techniques that he
or she should use in order to bring about a desired behavioral
result, and on the principles and procedures that the parent could
count on to regulate the behavior of the child."

Application Activities

1. Interview a professional in a community parenting or family life program
   about specific job duties and his outlook on the field of parent education.

2. List at least five (5) different program delivery systems and identify the
   type of professional readiness that would prepare one to work in the
   role.

3. Classify concepts relative to parents and education. Arrange them in
   some order of importance. Explain your reasons for order of priority.

4. Compare two different programs with regard for criteria of function,
   philosophy, population served, funding sources, and program goals.

5. Interview one parent who has used the services of a parent education
   program. Outline or discuss his reaction to the materials and information
   received, the convenience of the program, and his attitude toward participation in the program.

6. Discuss or outline several ways in which the federal government has
   supported education programs incorporating parents.

7. Interview one or two sets of parents who have not attended any form of
   education programs for parents. Determine what they perceive to be
   their most serious need in better family management. Ask them to list
   those needs in order of priority.

8. Interview an administrator of parenting courses. Obtain information about
   how the program originated (e.g., needs established, audience defined).

9. Design a hypothetical parent education course on any particular topic
   appropriate for parents.

10. Develop a parent survey and interview a minimum of 25 parents who use a public service. Ask what they consider to be their most serious problems with their children and whether or not they would be willing to attend parent education programs to explore these problems.

Bibliography

Beard, R.O. 1927. *Parent education*. Minneapolis, MN: The University of Minnesota Press.

Brim, O. 1959. *Education for child rearing*. New York: Russell Sage Foundation.

Bronfenbrenner, U. 1974. A Report and Longitudinal Evaluation of Pre-school Programs. Doc. #620-148/2160 1 – 3. Washington, D.C., U.S. Government Printing Office.

Brown, M.A.S. 1975. Education for parenthood, a new idea? *Forecast For Home Economics*, 20: F19.

Earhart, E.M. 1980. Parent education: A lifelong process. *Journal of Home Economics*. 72: 39 – 43.

Endres, M. and Evans, M. 1968. Some effects of parent education on parents and their children. *Adult Education Journal*, 18: 101 – 111.

Fantini, M., and Cardenas, R. (eds) 1980. *Parenting in a multicultural society*. New York: Longman.

Guttman, J.A. 1978. Getting parents involved in preschool. *The Education Digest*, 44: 15 – 18.

Hess, R.D. 1980. Experts and Amateurs! Some Unintended Consequences of Parent Education in *Parenting in a multicultural society*. New York: Longman.

Keniston, K. 1979. Children and families. *Journal of Home Economics*. 71: 14 – 16.

Kroth, R. 1978. Parents — powerful and necessary allies. *Teaching Exceptional Children*, 10: 88 – 90.

Luckey, E. 1977. Family life education. *Home Economics News,* 2: 1 – 4.

Magdid, T.D. (et. al.) 1979. Preparing pregnant teenagers for parenthood. *The Family Coordinator*, 28: 359 – 62.

Morrison, G.S. 1978. Parent involvement in the home, school, and community. Columbus, Ohio: Charles E. Merrill Publishing Co.

Nebgen, M.K. 1979. Parent involvement in Title I programs. *The Education Forum*. 43: 165 – 73.

Pierson, D.E., and Sperber, R.I. 1974. The Brookline Early Education Project: An issue for national educational policy. *Childhood Education*, 50: 132 – 35.

Stevens, J.H. Jr. 1978. Parent education programs: What determines effectiveness? *Young Children*, 33: 59 – 64.

Suchara, H.J. 1977. The child's right to humane treatment. *Childhood Education*, 53: 290 – 95.

White, B.L. 1977. *Guidelines for parent education*. Paper prepared for the Planning Conference, 29 September 1977, at Flint, Michigan.

White, B.L. 1980. The Year in Review. *Newsletter*. The Center for Parent Education, 55 Chapel St., Newton, Massachusetts 02160, Vol. 111, #1.

2. The Parent As a Model

Generalization

Weisz's (1980) suggestion that children are discerning observers of adults, particularly their parents, is well known. Most theories of socialization state that a child's behavior is based, in part, on modeling his parents' behavior.

Instrumental is the parents' impact on socializing the young child. The parental influence on young children can be compared with the young animal that must literally be trained in the ways of its owner; in other words, the young child must be taught the conditions, rules, and ways of his immediate family. Often this training is conducted through the use of words, but frequently the young child learns what to do by "watching and acting like" the parents. The intellectual influence, combined with the demonstrated behavior, shapes or socializes the child and results in a "modeling effect."

The most important function of the family in socialization is that it introduces the child to model-significant relationships.

Objectives

Chapter two provides the professional educator with a knowledge base relating to the importance of teaching parents about their dynamic modeling role and of providing a psychologically positive modeling environment for the young child. Objectives:

1. to review the literature for interpretations of contemporary parent roles and how they relate to socialization
2. to discuss the socialization process and explain the sex role identification variables that are important to parents
3. to consider the psychological concept of bonding and attachment and the importance of this concept in subsequent parent child interaction

4. to review values-development as it relates to the establishment of healthy parent-child relationships
5. to examine variables and methods for promoting positive self-esteem

Social roles are learned in the family through parental modeling. Roles copied are a prescribed way of acting so that fewer adjustments are necessary and life becomes more predictable. For the young child there are four inter-related processes that establish and strengthen identification with a model:

1. sharing physical or psychological attributes with the model
2. experiencing emotions similar to those of the model
3. wanting to be like the model
4. behaving like the model in play

Evaluations of young children often use low income families as the study populations. One study hypothesized that parents who have few modeling skills could break the cycle of ineffective behavior by observing acceptable modeling behavior themselves. This study by Goodman also suggested that if the mother's behavior can be modified, it might be a mediating step between application of the educators' knowledge and improved functioning on the part of the child.

The Significance: Attachment to Modeling

Attachment studies stress the importance of the mother and infant attachment and how it can influence later behaviors. Since maternal attachments occur early, eye contact with the infant is important; the eyes become a curious area for the infant to focus on. Eye-to-eye contact is a precursor to the human social smile and is important during a child's first six months of life. The amount of eye contact given to an infant should predict the intensity of the infant's tie to his mother. (Robson, 1976).

Moore (1977) believes that the most competent and precocious infants and children interact with parents who encourage them and keep their children's abilities and interests in mind. These indications of role and convergence suggest that mutual modeling occurs during early infancy.

The reciprocal relationship is evident as well, since infants become increasingly responsive to parent vocalization and smiles. Both mothers and fathers are sensitive and responsive to infant cues and are effective modifiers of infant behavior. Findings support a model of parent-infant interaction that stresses mutually regulating characteristics.

Sex Typing and Role Development

Sex typing, as described by Robinson and Hobson (1978), is a process by which adults help children acquire an understanding of their masculine and feminine sex identities. At birth, children have physical traits that distinguish them as either male or female, but their sex-role identity is not inborn. Powerful influences in the social environment emphasize or suppress sex characteristics of the developing child. Children are guided as to who they are and to the kinds of behavior other members of their society will find acceptable.

Another factor in sex-role development is imitation, the learning of one's sex role through observing and copying the behavior of a model. Children imitate the behavior of the same-sex adults who are around them. Encouraged to be masculine, a boy imitates a male model, including mannerisms, habits, values, and interests. Similarly, the observation of a female model results in a greater likelihood of feminine behavior in a girl. One's sexual identity parallels cognitive growth; it develops and changes through life. As children mature intellectually, they become more aware of how a male or female is expected to behave. Through a growing understanding, children learn appropriate sex roles and identify with them, thereby operating a process known as "self-socialization."

Role Appropriateness

According to Masters (1979), two important determinants of children's limitative learning and behavior are the sex of a model and the appropriateness of the modeled behavior relative to the sex of the child. The author suggests that social learning theorists have repeatedly noticed that a similarity between the child and the model enhances imitation. From this it can be argued that children should generally attend to and imitate their same sex parent more than the opposite sex parent because they perceive models who are the same sex to be more like themselves. It can be hypothesized that if a child witnessed a modeled behavior which was sex-appropriate for the sex of that child, regardless of the sex of the parent model, then that child would display a greater imitation than would a child of the opposite sex.

Assisting Children in Sex-Role Development

There are at least six ways parents and other caregivers can help to make the sex-typing process a successful experience.

Warm and Nurturant Relationships. Children acquire their sex-role identity best when adults are warm and nurturant, rather than punitive in their interactions with children. The adult's warm and rewarding attitude increases the child's desire to adopt the role of the same-sex parent.

Combining Affection and Dominance. Sex-role development is promoted when adults combine affection with dominance. Children of both sexes usually imitate the dominant parent more than the passive parent. When the father is dominant and affectionate, the son is more masculine. Boys from female-dominant homes tend to imitate their mothers and seem to be more passive than boys from male-dominant homes. Girls identify more with mothers who are dominant and affectionate. The best arrangement is for parents to share power since both parental warmth and parental dominance is important to children's sex-role identification. (Heatherington, 1965 and Heatherington and Frankie, 1967).

Providing Male and Female Models. The presence of both male and female models fosters sex-role development in the child. Children from father-absent or mother-absent homes may benefit from exposure to sex-role models as a substitute for the missing parent. Substitute models help children distinguish male roles from female roles. The presence of both female and male models helps children learn appropriate sex-role behavior and to understand role contrasts of the opposite sex.

Schools for young children are dominated by females. Therefore, it is desirable to recruit males into the classroom setting. Until the time more men can be employed in early childhood settings, volunteers could be integrated: retired men, local military men, local businessmen, male relatives, school workmen, and male students. Field trips to the places of employment of firemen, policemen, and other male-dominated occupations also give children more exposure to men. When possible, it would be helpful to have these men bring their tools of the trade to the classroom.

Developing Both Masculine and Feminine Traits. Children should be exposed to both masculine and feminine roles. They should be allowed to incorporate both masculine and feminine traits, which make them well-rounded human beings. Young children can be given some choices in experimenting with different roles: boys can play in the housekeeping area and help make snacks; girls can be allowed to play competitive games, do woodworking, or play with cars and trucks.

Accepting the Child's Biological Sex. Successful sex-role development is closely tied to the feelings children have toward themselves. It is important that the adults in children's lives accept them for who they are and never say anything like, "I wish you had been a boy (girl)." Adult acceptance builds self-esteem in the child. Generally, children who have good self-esteem have acquired their sex roles easily.

Questions: Human Sexuality. Sometimes it is necessary for the teacher to provide sex education. Children are curious; they ask questions about parts of the body or bodily functions. Clear, honest explanations should be given, using correct terms rather than slang words.

Preschool children are around female adults most of the time, so boys frequently must infer their appropriate sex-role behavior. Lynn and Cross (1970) suggested that this inferential behavior may cause pre-school boys to be unsure of their sex identities.

Sex-typing is the process of helping children obtain an understanding of masculine and feminine sex roles. Parents are significantly important in determining the degree of sex-typing their children receive and follow because children tend to imitate the same sex adult model. Parents need to display consistency in their nonverbal behavior as well as in their verbal communication and as role models of young children; parents must not contradict themselves.

Characteristics of the model and characteristics of the situation (Thomas, 1973) are two factors that help determine whether or not a child will imitate a particular response. Much research supports the contention that children will more often imitate a live model, either a peer or an adult, as compared with a cartoon or other non-human model. Children respond more to examples of behavior than to preaching about behavior. Another characteristic which appears to be important is the personality of the model. Pederson (1979) has concluded that the father is a significant component in the early environment and many times one hears of the need to have male pre-school and primary school teachers so that boys will have access to a role model in school. Similarly, requests are made for teachers from minority groups so that minority group children will be able to identify with the teacher. Nevertheless, although conclusive results are not yet available, it appears that a warm teacher, particularly one who rewards children appropriately, is influential as a model regardless of race or sex (Thelen, 1971).

Reinforcement

Direct rewards, or reinforcement, are important in imitation learning and desired rewards may serve to bring attention to the relevant modeling cues. It is also suggested that reward may be developmentally and differentially effective, particularly with younger children. Positive versus negative rewards have been studied in relationship to imitation learning. One study was conducted using positive, negative, and neutral feedback with a major finding to be the "halo effect" of positive outcomes. If the model received at least some positive rewards, it appeared to be more effective than a negative reward or no reward at all in establishing certain behaviors. The history of reinforcement as well as the expectations of the subject are also important variables to be covered in the reinforcement process.

Mother's Role

In Pasqualis' (1978) study, responses of 104 female adolescents were analyzed to determine the influence of the mother's place of work, at home or away, and the influence of the mother's job satisfaction on the daughter's sex-role identification. Results showed that the satisfaction the mother gained from her job was an important factor in the daughter's positive sexual identification, but the mother's place of work had no influence on the daughter's sexual identification.

Barrett (1979) investigated forty-four families enrolled in a family counseling clinic near Pittsburgh, Pennsylvania. Based on interviews and personal observations, he found that the quality of the relationship between the mother and the father had the most impact on the mother's relationship with her child. If a woman has someone to provide her with emotional support and to make her feel important, she is better able to pass along these positive feelings to her child.

Father's Role

One analysis showed that being a single father required major shifts in life styles and priorities for most men. The more traditional spheres of male functioning at work and in social life were redefined and organized by focusing on the bond between the parent and child. The men appeared to limit their work and social activities to meet the needs of their children and, in doing so, developed closer relationships with their children. The experience of a marital separation forced these men to be responsible for their children's growth and satisfying the children's needs. Some men responded by restructuring their daily lives to care directly for their dependent children. As a result, according to Schlesinger (1978), the fathers felt more positive about themselves as parents and as individuals. A majority of men reported that they had become more responsive to their children and more conscious of their needs, a responsiveness they reported as reaching out to other adults as well.

Male Models

In one study, comparisons were made between the expectation patterns of the males in this sample and those of their own fathers. The results indicated a significant trend away from traditional expectations for the younger generation of males. However, when these males were compared with their contemporary females, the males were far more traditional, an attitudinal lag which may cause disagreements in future mother-father dyads. The males did seem to be changing their expectations about what a father should be, but the changes were not as rapid as those made by the females (Eversall, 1979).

Three researchers at the University of Toronto found that gender identity problems for biological males were often accompanied by the loss of the father. The psychological literature up to that time had given minimal importance to the father and maximum importance to the mother-child relationship. In this study it was found that fathers were important, especially in gender identity formation. A man's fathering style can be influenced by factors other than his own father's style; for instance, it is modeled partly after the style of interaction he experiences in his daily occupation.

Self-Esteem and Modeling

Self-esteem consists of the thoughts, feelings, and ideas a person has about himself. It is his overall judgment of himself, how much a person likes, accepts, and respects himself. In one way or another, most of the things children and parents do are directly related to feelings about self. The friends one chooses, how one relates to others, the type of person one marries, one's creativity, one's achievement, and one's basic personality are all affected by a person's concept of himself. In other words, strong self-esteem is not only the foundation of sound mental health but also is influential in developing the attitudes and values that will contribute to a happy life. As such, the building of a good self-image in children is undoubtedly one of the greatest challenges of parenthood.

The author hypothesizes that self-esteem is positively related to the closeness of the parent-child relationship. She further asserts that a boy's self-esteem is closely associated with his relationship to his father whereas a girl's self-concept is closely correlated with her relationship to her mother.

Self-Esteem Assumptions

A person's self-esteem is related to:

1. how he is treated by others
2. his history of successes and failures
3. his physical, social, and mental abilities
4. how he interprets his experiences and his manner of responding to them
5. his expectations for himself and other peoples' expectations for him
6. heredity-temperament

A child's self-concept (the picture of who he is and what he can do) is learned. By the time the child is five or six years old he has a fairly clear picture of "who he is." Feelings of self-worth can and do change with experiences and over time.

Behavior generally matches a person's self-image. One of the causes of misbehavior is a negative self-concept.

A person's feelings of self-worth affect all aspects of his life: the friends he chooses, his academic and professional success, family relationship, creativity, and relationships with others. In addition, verbal and non-verbal communication is one of the most important influences on a person's self-esteem. Humans are not born with high or low self-esteem. A person's feelings about himself are learned, beginning at birth and continuing throughout his life. Experiences in the formative first few years of life constitute the foundation of one's feelings about himself; then the feelings are constantly revised, positively or negatively, following additional experiences. A high level of self-esteem is possible for any person since it is not linked to a family's wealth, education, or social class. It is reactive to the quality of the relationship that exists between a person and others significant in his life. For a child, a sense of worth is nurtured by the family members closely involved in his care or by people who provide day care. As the child grows older, the school joins in influencing a child's feelings about himself.

A child's self-esteem is also related to his assessment of how he "measures up" to what people expect. When a child's expectations are realistic, it is easy for him to experience success and feel personally valuable, thereby building his self-esteem. On the other hand, when his expectations are too high or rigid, he may be dissapointed; and as disappointments mount, his view of his own value and his self-esteem may diminish.

Assessment of Self-Concept

According to some theories, an assessment of self-concept can be accomplished by observing the child in daily interactions and by using the simple rating scale of "Always," "Usually," "Sometimes," "Seldom,'" or "Never" for the following questions:

1. Does the child adopt easily to new situations?
2. Does the child hesitate to express himself?
3. Does the child become upset by failures or stressful situations?
4. Do other children seek out the child to engage in activities?
5. Does the child become alarmed or frightened easily?
6. When the child is scolded or criticized, does he become either aggressive or withdrawn?
7. Does the child frequently indicate that he does not do as well as others expect him to do or as well as he expects himself to do?
8. Does the child tend to dominate or bully other children?
9. Does the child continually seek attention by speaking out of turn, boasting, making unnecessary noises, or by displaying other inappropriate behavior?
10. Does the child appear to approve and accept the performance of his body?

Antecedents to Self-Esteem

Evidence from one study suggested that the most notable antecedents of high self-esteem were directly related to parent behavior and the consequences of the rules and regulations that parents establish for their children. Definite and consistently enforced limits on behaviors were associated with high self-esteem. Families that produced children who had high self-esteem exerted greater demands upon them for academic performance and excellence. Parents with high self-esteem accepted their children, and parents who expected their children to live up to the standards they established were more likely to facilitate healthy growth in their children than parents who did not establish any standards to be met. It is important to note that there are not patterns of behavior common to all parents with children of high self-esteem but rather, a combination of the above factors is necessary to produce high self-esteem.

Several interpersonal patterns emerge among parents with low self-esteem. Their relationships are stressful and sometimes the result is that the children have problems with their own self-esteem:

- Parents with low self-esteem tend to "live through their chidren." They want their children to achieve goals they have not achieved and they are disappointed if the children fail.

- Parents with low self-esteem are often anxious, which distorts communication. As a result, they do not hear their children accurately and they give ambiguous or contradictory messages.

- Parents with low self-esteem are often threatened if their children have high self-esteem, particularly if the children seek independence and autonomy.

- When parents have low self-esteem they see most things as problems or potential problems and attempt to divert problems that may not even exist.

- Parents with low self-esteem have difficulty praising children realistically and precisely. They tend to praise seldom or to praise to excess.

- Parents with low self-esteem tend to convey mixed messages about success to their children. They encourage their children to be successful, but also imply that success will be short-lived. (Bean and Clemes, 1978)

Enhancing Self-Esteem

1. Respond to each child individually and call him by name.

2. Take time to talk with the child about what is important *to him*.

3. Use positive guidance and suggestions whenever possible. Reinforce the behavior you like.

4. Be realistic and make *your expectations* consistent with the *child's* stage of development and ability.

5. Give the child an opportunity to make choices and have responsibilities that fit his stage of development.

6. Provide opportunities for the child to succeed, and challenge him when the chances for success are good.

7. Give a child "quality" time as opposed to "quantity" time.

8. Compare a child's skills to his previous accomplishments, but avoid comparing him to other children, especially brothers or sisters.

9. Avoid shaming or labeling a child.

10. Be a good model because children learn by watching adults.

11. React to the child's behavior instead of to the child personally. ("I don't want the living room cluttered with all your toys" instead of "you're a messy, bad boy"). Use "I" versus "you" messages.

12. Give a child recognition for his accomplishments.

13. Accept the child's negative and positive feelings without judging him.

14. Establish reasonable limits.

15. Show warmth when you greet or say farewell and welcome each child into the group so that he feels like a member.

16. Help children succeed in important areas of growth: developing a basic trust, achieving autonomy, and demonstrating initiative. Provide opportunities for children to explore, to get first-hand experiences, and to learn how to control negative impulses.

17. Help children learn to acknowledge and verbalize feelings in constructive ways.

18. Remember, a child who is "misbehaving" needs approval and acceptance.

19. Be aware of the verbal and non-verbal "messages" you send to children.

20. Be careful not to show "favoritism" or to treat children differently with respect to praise, feedback, criticism, encouragement, or help. (Be mindful of children who are slow to learn).

The Origin
Many researchers have defined these behaviors as typical of children with global positive self-concepts:

1. He is unafraid of a new situation.

2. He makes friends with other children easily.

3. He experiments easily with new materials.

4. He trusts his teacher even though she is a stranger to him.

5. He is cooperative and can usually follow reasonable rules.

6. He is largely responsible for controlling his own behavior.

7. He is creative, imaginative, and has ideas of his own.

8. He talks freely and may have difficulty listening to others.

9. He is independent and needs only a minimum amount of help or direction from his teacher.

10. He seems, for the most part, to be a happy individual.

Typical Behaviors: Low Self-Concept

1. He seldom shows initiative.

2. He relies on others for direction.

3. He asks permission to do anything.

4. He seldom shows spontaneity.

5. He seldom enters new activities.

6. He isolates himself.

7. He talks very little.

8. He is possessive of objects.

9. He makes excessive demands.

10. He withdraws or aggresses.

11. He reacts with signs of frustration.
    (Survant, 1972)

Values and Moral Development

Accepting the traditional values and customs of their community can give stability to families, friends, and neighbors. However, parents may also pass on to their children attitudes that prevent them from accepting and appreciating differences in others, such as religion, race, or wealth. Parents must decide which values are worthy of transmitting to their children. One test is to question whether or not the values being imparted will help the children respect themselves and the rights of others.

Children are keen observers, and parents should exhibit in their daily living the values they want their children to learn. Moralities are systems of rules that are external to people, designed to guide social or interpersonal behavior. Moral behavior consists of actions carried out with regard to the rules that apply in a given social context, and moral character is defined in terms of those dispositions and traits that are subject to moral evaluation within a society. In a sense, all education is moral for it seeks to bring about excellence in the young. Early moral education helps young people develop moral sensitivity without becoming complete moral skeptics. Within the framework of three of our major institutions — family, school, and religion — parents desperately try to separate the important from the trivial, but often it is their heightened confusion that they pass directly to their children.

Cultural values and attitudes are communicated informally to children, especially as children watch adults' reactions to particular events. Young children appear to be influenced by what they see others doing and the rewards that behavior receives, In an experimental setting, altruism is a value often used as the modeled behavior. Bryan, Redfield, and Mader (1971) studied second and third grade children who heard a model either exhort greed or charity, or verbalize about neutral material. Following exposure to the model, half of the children in each group received social reinforcements from the model for responses minimizing material rewards. The model who practiced and preached charity and rewarded self-denial responses elicited the greatest number of self-denial responses from the children.

In another study, first grade children who observed the sharing behavior of a very generous adult model later shared more than children who had observed the behavior of a very stingy model (Presbie & Coiteux, 1971). Results of most studies of altruism, sharing, and generosity indicate the strong effects of observed behavior, particularly when compared with preaching or exhortation.

It appears that parent identification is related to conscience development, and includes the recognition that moral principles rather than external sanctions are used for the basis of right and wrong.

Morals are behaviors that conform to the customs or standards of certain codes. Ethics is sometimes confused with morality in that it refers more directly to human behavior in a philosophical sense. Morality usually surfaces during the adolescent period when young people gain an understanding of why certain things are right or wrong. Morality must be linked with guilt in order to motivate a child to conform. To feel guilt, a child must first accept the standards of right and wrong, good and bad, as his own. He must also be able to regulate his behavior according to these standards and feel accountable if he fails to. Morality is learned; a child learns what his parents believe to be right and wrong. A moral foundation is laid before a child associates with people outside of his family.

At birth, a child is pre-moral; he begins life incapable of moral judgments and moral behavior. As a neonate, the child is bound only by sensations and impulses but eventually learns his culture and becomes "moral." Moral development is one part of total social development. It is oriented toward the priority of values and the concepts of rights and responsibilities in relation to social situations and social environments. For education purposes, parents should be aware that children develop morally as they develop socially. If parents have a significant influence on the socialization process, then they will be equally influential in the determination of moral behavior.

Parents accept a child who knows nothing; they teach him how to be social. It is assumed that learning to be social is also learning to be moral. The acceptability or unacceptability of the social or moral concepts is determined by the culture, or the thought characteristics, of a community.

According to Williams & Fey (1980), providing education about morality does not provide the values themselves. The education is teaching the process of reaching moral decisions. In a study seeking to determine whether adolescents acquire their values from their parents or from their peers, the conclusion reached was that students held values closer to those of their peers than to those of their parents. Since individuals do not acquire their values solely from their parents, it is difficult for parents to influence their children to acquire values that parents deem acceptable. Parents should not force values on a child; a child has a mind of his own and should be allowed the freedom to make his own choice as to which values he wants to accept and which he wants to reject.

Values clarification begins with the observation that individuals and societies are suffering from many problems, not the least of which are values. In individual lives, the symptoms of value confusion are apathy, flightiness, over-conformity, over-dissention, and a lack of perceived purpose — a state of confusion, anguish, or suffering. An individual's value problems can also affect his relationships, contribute to considerable conflict within families and groups, and lead to inefficiency and a reduction of constructive activity in society.

Values Clarification

Values clarification is an intervention technique consisting of questions, a set of activities or "strategies," and an approach toward subject content, all of which are designed to help individuals learn a particular valuing process and apply that process to value-laden areas and moral dilemmas. Use of the valuing process helps individuals develop and clarify their values in such a way that they experience positive value in their own lives and act more constructively in the social context. Research and theory in the areas of moral reasoning, critical thinking, creativity and problem-solving, attitude change, self-concept, psychotherapy, achievement motivation, group dynamics, helping relationships, and skill training have grown rapidly in the last few decades (Kirchenbaum, et al., 1977).

Teaching Values

One mother says, "I have become so tolerant that I am no longer sure what values I want to pass onto my children. Everything seems so mixed up with different causes and reasons. Nothing seems clear anymore. If I do not know what to believe, how can I clarify things for my seven year old? How can I answer the many questions she asks about why people do the things they do?" (Jenkins, 1979)

Traditional values and behavior can give stability to families and aid in developing a cohesive group of friends and neighbors who understand one another.

It is at this point that parents have to make some decisions of their own. They must think about their own personal values and select those they really want to share with their children. Here we must answer the questions — what is right and what is wrong? Our children are growing up in a world already different from the one we grew up in. They must learn to live and work with many different kinds of people and to make decisions in situations we have never had to meet. What values will they need in this changing world? A clue to sound action mght be to ask ourselves if the values we are passing to our children are those that will help them to respect themselves and the rights of other people, or will result in either physical or psychological harm to themselves or others (Jenkins, 1978).

In a democratic country such as ours, children need to learn to think and they need to like to think. Thinking for oneself is an important value to cultivate; without thought, the problems of living together cannot be easily solved. As children grow, they must learn to think for themselves in order to solve problems and cope with the experiences life will bring to them. As they begin to use their own judgment and make their own decisions, children will rely upon the values their parents gave them.

For centuries man passed on his moral code in hope of preserving his most cherished values and attitudes. Our culture is going through a transition in which institutions are re-evaluating their goals and values. This is positive because it helps people to re-examine themselves and decide what issues are major or minor in relation to their life styles. There was a lapse in moral education until it was realized how important it is to everyday living. It provides a base upon which decisions are made. Moral values reflect society and can serve as an indicator of what trends in attitudes may be on the rise or decline. Probably the most significant reason for research is to find out how moral attitudes and values affect everyday living, why they affect our lives, how are these beliefs and attitudes best taught, and how to translate findings into teachable concepts.

Responsibility and Moral Behavior

Jensen and Hughston (1979) list below the techniques which a parent may use to promote responsibility and moral behavior.

1. be positive and predictable

2. minimize mistakes

3. listen to children

4. model the behavior you expect children to exhibit

5. respect yourself as well as the child

6. allow children to make choices

7. set limits

8. create feelings of adequacy

9. promote autonomy

Directions for Using Moral Decision-Making Situations

A series of situations will be found on the following pages. Imagine you are the mother or father of the child described. All the children in the following situations are to be considered six years old.

Write down, in a word, sentence, or short paragraph, how you would respond to the child in each of the situations. Write down your exact words and actions as if you were writing a movie script, but please do not explain *why* you said or did what you described.

A. Introduce the dilemma by defining the terms and the nature of it.

B. Help parents establish their individual positions on the action.

C. Select the appropriate strategy for grouping the parents. There may be small groups of parents who agree on the action but for different reasons, or there may be small groups of parents who do not agree on the action. Examine the likenesses or differences among the groups.

D. Ask students to summarize the different reasons that they have heard.

E. Ask parents if they believe there is a best answer for this problem.

F. Add any additional reasons that did not occur from parent discussions; these should not be added as the "best" reasons but as additional reasons to ponder.

Situations

1. You and your spouse are both going out for the evening. As you are leaving you both say "good night" to your son, Frank. He cries and pleads with you both not to go and leave him alone, even though he does not appear to be sick and he has gotten along well with the babysitter in the past.

2. Your daughter, Barbara, has just come home from school; she is silent, sad-faced, and dragging her feet. You can tell by her manner that something unpleasant has happened to her.

3. Before going to bed at 10 p.m., you go into your son Bert's bedroom to see if he has a blanket over him and to tuck him in, if necessary. You find that he is awake and is masturbating. He sees you looking at him and as you approach him he stops and pulls the blanket up to his chin.

4. You have completed shopping in a local supermarket and as you are checking out, your son Lee says he wants a candy bar. It is nearly dinner time so you say, "No," to his request. He then lies down and screams and kicks at you.

Application Activities

1. Identify three values you would like to pass on to your children. Discuss these three values with a group of peers. Are their values similar or different?

2. Read a story based on a moral issue and design and role-play a moral dilemma activity.

3. Using McDonald's informed assessment, observe four children at play and complete the rating scale.

4. Interview two parents who have children in kindergarten. Using Survant's definition of Global Self-Concept, determine if these children have high or low global self-concept.

5. Describe three ways a mother or father might act to enhance self-esteem in their child.

6. Develop a "Feelings" learning center.
   A. Creative writing: Use pictures of people as stimuli for children to write about how the person in the picture feels and why the person might feel that way.
   B. Graphing: Have children take a survey about what makes people angry, happy, or sad. Graph the results.

7. Make a list of rules appropriate for children in the home. Describe why you think these rules are important.

8. Form a discussion group with several sets of parents. Explore with them their feelings regarding their child's self-concept:
   A. Have them complete McDonald's informed assessment or Survant's Global Self-Concept definition in reference to their child.
   B. Assist the parents in identifying components of positive and negative self-concept.
   C. Explore ideas and methods to enhance self-concept in the home.

9. Explore the concept of self-esteem as it relates to culture. Identify how self-esteem is fostered in the upper, middle, and lower classes. Describe appropriate means to enhance self-esteem within each of these environments.

10. Attend a preparation for childbirth class for first-time parents. Ask them to describe what they expect a newborn's behavior to be like. Identify "roadblocks" to realistic expectations. Describe a method you might use in assisting parents in defining more realistic behaviors for their children.

11. Interview one or several social workers in a children's service agency to collect their opinions on causal factors in the negative or positive socialization of young children. Synthesize these into a generalized statement with references.

12. Observe a nursery school class and describe patterns of play that are common for boys, common for girls, and common for both boys and girls. Identify ways in which the nursery school curriculum and environment might be changed to enhance sex equity.

13. Interview a rabbi, a priest, and a Protestant minister to learn their techniques for promoting moral development in children:
   A. How are the techniques similar or different?
   B. What do they consider to be moral or immoral behaviors?
   C. To what degree do the varying religious philosophies affect their definitions of moral behavior?

Bibliography

Barnett, M.A. et. al. 1979. Empathy in young children: Relationship to parents' empathy. *Affection, and Emphasis on the Feelings of Others,* ERIC Document ED 176 – 898.

Bean, R., and Clemes, H. 1978. Raising children's self-esteem. *A Handbook for Parents.* Association for Personal and Organizational Development. 1427 41st Ave., Capitola, California 95010.

Bryan, J.H., Redfield, J., Mader, S. 1971. Words and deeds about altruism and the subsequent reinforcement power of the model. *Child Development,* 42: 1401 – 508.

Eversall, D. 1979. The changing father role: Implications for parent education programs for today's youth. *Adolescence.* 14: 535 – 43.

Goodman, E.O. Jr. 1965. Modeling: A method of parent education. *The Family Coordinator,* 24: 7 – 11.

Heatherington, E.M. 1965. A developmental study of the effects of sex of the dominant parent on sex-role preference, identification, and imitation in children. *Journal of Personality and Social Psychology,* 2: 188 – 94.

Heatherington, E.M., 1967. Effects of parental dominance, warmth, and conflict on imitation in children. *Jouranl of Personality and Social Psychology,* 2: 188 – 94.

Jenkins, G.G. 1978. For parents particularly. *Childhood Education.* 55: 22 – 24.

Kirschenbaum, H., et. al. 1977 In defense of values clarification. *Phi Delta Kappan,* 58: 743 – 46.

Lynn, D.B., and Cross, A.R. 1970. Parent preference of preschool children, ED 041 628.

Masters, J.C. 1979. Modeling and labeling as integrated determinants of children's sex-typed initiative behavior. *Child Development,* 50: 364.

Moore, S. 1977. Research in review: Mother child interaction and competence in infants and toddlers. *Young Children,* 32: 64 – 69. ·

Pasquali, L. , and Callegari, A.I. 1978. Working mothers and daughters' sex-role identification in Brazil. *Child Development,* 49: 902 – 05.

Pedersen, F.A., Rubenstein, J.L., and Yarrow, L.J. 1979. Infant development in father-absent families. *The Journal of Genetic Psychology,* 135: 51 – 61.

Presbie, R.J., and Coiteux, P.F. 1971. Learning to be generous or stingy: Imitation of sharing behavior as a function of model generosity and vicarious reinforcement. *Child Development.* 42: 1033 – 038.

Robson, K. 1976. The role of eye to eye contact in maternal-infant attachment. *Child and Family*, 15: 119 – 32.

Schlesinger, B. 1978. Single parent: A research review. *Children Today*, 8:
12 – 17.

Survant, A. 1972. Building positive self-concepts. *Instructor*, 81: 94 – 95.

Thelen, M.H. 1971. The effect of subject race, model race, and vicarious
praise on vicarious learning. *Child Development*. 42: 972 – 77.

Thomas, S. 1973. Modeling and imitation learning in young children. An
Abstract Bibiliography. ERIC University of Illinois at Urbana Champaign,
805 W. Pennsylvania Avenue, Urbana, Illinois 61801.

Williams, D., and Fey, C. 1980. Moral education: every teacher's responsibility and reward. *American Secondary Education*, 7: 15 – 20.

3. "Parenting" Education

Generalization

The purpose of parenting education or education for parenthood is to assist parents in becoming skilled in the application of child development principles and to offer ways in which this new knowledge can improve the parent's respect for the child rearing process. The interpretation that goes into this process and the environment in which the process occurs are also important topics.

Social mobility, concentration on the nuclear family, and an increase in child abuse reinforce the necessity of informing adults about how children develop, about the particular variables that enhance a child's growth, and about resources to enhance the family setting. While many family life education programs for parents have varied contents, the programs that engage child development and parent-child interaction skills are the most traditional and are considered educational. (Lavack and Ries, 1978). Parents are not trained to be parents and as a result, they need to understand the norms and management principles of growth and development to be able to perform with more positive mental and physical health strategies.

As Brim (1959) and Beard (1927) pointed out, we as a society "provide little or no opportunity for parents to consider, sort, and integrate pertinent information;" yet, "the family absorbs much of the blame for most of our social problems," and it is the family then that "must adapt to the demands of a highly mechanized economic system." Of all the responsibilities people are called upon to undertake in life, it is hard to imagine one more perplexing and more demanding— a more rigorous test of wisdom, patience, and judgment under pressure— than that of being a parent. Nor are there many responsibilities for which most people are less prepared. There is no doubt that the family provides the most significant psychological and physical socialization process for each child; therefore, the family setting is the most appropriate place to establish a sound and positive mental health base. All of us have seen and experienced the results of nonenhancing family mental health.

Objectives

To assist the professional student in interpreting the component of child development for parents, the objectives will be:

1. to explain the rationale for the child development content for teaching parents

2. to identify specific program approaches for teaching principles of child development to parents

3. to choose those child development concepts suitable for use with parents

4. to illustrate specific ways the parents can ultimately establish positive family environments

5. to discuss the importance of and strategies to reinforce the communicating process in parent-child relationships and interactions

6. to discuss ways to enrich psychological and maintenance strengths that parents naturally possess

7. to isolate discipline as the most significant problem area and interpret it from a perspective that a parent educator would find useful when working with parents

8. to reinforce the medium of play as the most appropriate outlet for parent-child management situations

History and Roles

Historically, the idea of education for parenthood was discussed in Plato's *Republic*. In this country, organized approaches to the subject date back more than 100 years. National voluntary organizations such as the Child Study Association of America and the National Congress of Parents and Teachers have been leaders since the late nineteenth century. Programs that have paid particular attention to parent education have been government-funded. The people involved in these programs have been convinced that children can be helped by helping their parents. The person to work with parents should be someone who knows a lot about child-raising and education. Parent education is defined as having all types of activities and experiences that provide information and guidelines for the parent role (Earhart, 1980). The parent educator should be a resource to teachers as well as to parents and schools.

Related parent education and social service agencies should establish reinforcement systems to encourage parents to participate in the educator's offerings.

Approaches

There are at least two schools of thought as to how an adult can successfully learn the role of being a parent. One approach is that becoming mature, adjusted, wise, and patient will help an adult meet the problems of parenthood. An adult may achieve self-understanding, emotional poise, and maturity through group guidance or individual counseling. The basis of this school of thought is that parent education is achieved through psychotherapy.

The second approach to learning how to be a parent is that one can confront the problems of parenthood just as one might confront problems of learning in any area. As such, a person may learn fundamental facts and conditions that appear to promote mental and physical health in children (Handorf, 1978). This approach is considered educational in that the parent consciously enters into the education environment because he seeks knowledge or skills, as opposed to being considered therapeutic whereby the subconscious motions of the parent are explored.

Brim (1959) and Beard (1927) are perhaps the two theorists most associated with the concept of teaching parents about child development and child rearing techniques. It is assumed that this "science" helps parents become better parents, so to speak, and in so doing has long range benefits for family life.

Parent education offerings are designed to give factual information to parents. Many parents resolve some problems directly with factual information that is appropriately presented. For instance, when a parent learns that only about 50 percent of the study children are toilet trained before two years of age, the parent frequently reduces his own expectations of his child's toilet training program.

Some believe that entering into formal or informal education settings will cause parents to become anxious. Graston (1978), however, suggests that the body of information from years of scientific study of children and adults is availabe in many places and can be studied mucl. the same way as any other facts about children and their interpersonal- intrapersonal relationships skills. Gaston believes this does not increase parents' anxieties or cause them despair. And while parent education can be carried on profitably by individuals, there is a benefit to be derived by group study and group discussion, especially discussion led by trained local leaders.

The skills of being good parents have traditionally been passed from parents to children and have developed over the generations into a part of the culture. It appears lately, however, that home-centered life which once afforded children years to observe the art of being a parent as practiced by their parents is now a rarity; it seems to have been replaced by a complex and fragmented family life that offers little chance for apprenticeship. To combat this trend, people must be taught. Factual information will help parents recognize differences in maturity among children and how the differences affect children's interests, learning, play, and many other stages of childhood development and behavior. But there is evidence that all too many people are approaching parenthood with a dangerous lack of knowledge and skill concerning developmental aspects and other equally important areas of nutrition, self-concept, attitudes, and values. This inadequacy denies children parents who know how to do a good job of raising their children. (Graston, 1978).

Government Support

The objective of the Education for Parenthood or "Parenting" Programs is to break the cycle of parents knowing very little about raising children. Despite commitment to the concept of preparation for parenthod, federal agencies do not want to get involved in setting overall policy and designing complete programs. Much of the government's participation is coordinating and funding the programs. The decisions of what to include in the program and at what grade level they should be presented is left up to schools and respective social service agencies. In parenting, the social revolution means replacement of the autocratic philosophy of being a parent with the democratic philosophy of raising children. In the autocratic method, the parent was an enforcer; in the permissive style, the parent was submissive. In contrast, the democratic parent-child process is based on mutual respect, equality, freedom, and responsibility. The democratic process refers to human worth, dignity, and recognition.

Content

Since there is no expert advice on child-rearing, guidelines to "successful" parenthood should be developed. To implement such a plan of action, the task is to encourage the curious mind, to value the dignity of children, and to nurture humaneness (Romatowski, 1976).

Education for Parenthood

Parent education courses have varied over the years according to theoretical frameworks, topics, and presentation formats, but parents still have a wide choice of courses. Parents should be trained in many areas; besides child development, they should know what constitutes sound nutrition, balanced diet, and good prenatal health care (Bell, 1979; O'Connel, 1976).

Approaches

Programs should emphasize active parent involvement in all phases of the learning experience, from participation in discussions and activities to planning and leading sessions. Activities for the home, which parent participants can engage in with their children, are also stressed.

A key part of the program should be documentation— a journal in which parents can keep notes about their at-home activities. They can jot down observations of their children and any ideas, thoughts, and feelings that relate to their personal growth and development. The journal is used throughout the program in many settings and gives the parents an ongoing record of experiences that they can refer to and add to even after the program is complete.

Films are used to demonstrate observation and analysis skills. Recorded case studies give parents an opportunity to listen to and discuss the experiences of other parents involved in problem-solving situations. Brainstorming and role-plays are techniques by which parents are able to share ideas and experiences what someone else feels in a given situation.

As a result of parenting training, one study asked parents to comment on any changes in home atmosphere and in parent-child interactions. A content analysis was made of the written comments and the frequency of different types of responses was recorded. Expected outcomes could be:

1. an increase in the handling of a behavioral problem at its onset
2. an increase in the parents' awareness of the factors influencing their children's behavior
3. an increase in the parents' use of reinforcement for desirable child behavior, and
4. an increase in the parents' confidence in dealing with their children. It appears that parents can be effectively taught to use behavioral principles of child management by means of classroom procedures

Success of Parent Training

Wilson (1979) points out that there is a great deal of literature dealing with parent training, but the amount of training that is attempted, how much the training really meets the parents' needs, and what the outcomes of the training are remains questionable. Further, parent training should be analyzed from three perspectives:

1. research to confirm the efficiency of parent training
2. assessment of skills that trainers should have to meet the needs of each parent, and
3. a comparison of training programs and goals to assist parents in developing a program

Parents should be asked to evaluate their laboratory experiences and determine how well the experiences met their needs of gaining information about child development and encountering problems with their children. Most parents should see that working in the laboratory with their children is a worthwhile educational experience. It is beneficial in the sense of the parent-child encounter but it is also worthwhile for parents to meet other parents and just sit and talk about the hassles of raising children. It is a relief sometimes to know that other children go through similar stages or cause similar anxieties for their parents.

Recent Systems

Over the past twenty years, new program development efforts to assist parents in managing their children and families have given direction to systems that educate for the prevention of maladaptive behavior. The content of these systems has centered around improving the communication between parents and children so that self-concept, mental health, and ego stability of the child, as well as the parent, can be preserved. Major strategies for raising children are distinct from others that have appeared within the last fifteen years:

1. the democratic approach (Driekurs, 1958)
2. the humanistic approach (Ginott, 1965)
3. the parent-effectiveness strategy (Gordon, 1970), and
4. the transactional analysis approach (Berne, 1961, 1964)

The usefulness of these lie in their being effective, but they are not absolute methods for guiding parent-child interactions.

Gordon's Parent Effectiveness Strategy

Parent Effectiveness Training (PET), like other strategies, has many significant features that achieve a better result in the areas of communicating and interacting with children. The major features are explained below:

1. The parent acts as a counselor when a child has a problem and, in situations, PET involves the use of active listening. The way this is applied to a parent-child relation is that a child may come to the parent complaining of some particular problem or difficulty. The parent feeds back only what he or she understands the child to mean through the communications. The objective here is for the parent to understand and reflect back to the child what it is that is troubling the child. By employing active listening, the parent does not solve the child's problem because it is still the child's responsibility to search for solutions through the opportunity provided by the parent as an interested but objective party. For example, a child comes to his dad complaining that nobody wants to play with him.

   Dad: Why aren't you playing with the other kids?
   Boy: Nobody wants to play with me.
   Dad: You feel that you don't have any friends and that makes you feel bad?
   Boy: Yeah. I hate Tommy and all the others.
   Dad: You just hate all of them.
   Boy: Yeah. Especially Tommy.
   Dad: He's the worst?
   Boy: That's right. He makes fun of me and calls me names. I don't always throw the ball right.
   Dad: You get along better with Tommy if he doesn't call you names?
   Boy: You bet. I'm his friend but I don't like to be called names.
   Dad: You think you're Tommy's friend, and friends should be nice to each other.
   Boy: Yeah. Friends help each other. Maybe I can ask Tommy to show me how to throw the ball better, then he won't call me names.

   The father did not place himself in the position of preaching, admonishing, moralizing, or degrading his son for his feelings and he did not offer solutions for the child's problem. He did recognize the child's feelings of hurt and rejection. The encounter showed the child that he could reach his own insights with the helpful guidance of the father.

2. Not all interactions between parents and children require the parent to fulfill a therapeutic role. There are frequent occasions when the child's

behavior is a problem for the parents. The child usually does not view his behavior as troublesome even if the parent perceives it that way. In such situations, Gordon suggests that parents should be more assertive and use "I" messages to communicate their feelings to children. "I" messages are used to get children to listen to parents and they differ from the "you" messages that parents send in communications with children. Notice from the last section on active listening that the rater used many sentences starting with "you." These messages indicated that the father was listening to the child's communications. When "I" messages are used, however, the parent signals the child that he is to listen to the parent, for example, "I can't work well if you continue to bang on the piano." These messages communicate facts and help a child to modify the behavior that is unacceptable to the parent. "I" messages are less likely to promote resistance and rebellion from children, and they place the responsibility for changing the child's behavior on the child rather than on the parent.

3. When conflicts cannot be avoided, Gordon (1970) suggests that parents should use the "no-lose" method of conflict resolution in which the parent and the child reach a compromise.

Berne's Transactional Analysis Strategy

According to the Transactional Analysis (TA) theory, an individual has three egostates of his personality, each of which is seen as being a separate entity within the personality that guides interactions with and reactions to others. The first ego state to be developed by an individual is the child. This part of the personality psychologically records the feelings and heightened emotional states of our humanity, such as "creativity, intuition, and spontaneous drive and enjoyment" (Berne, 1964). The second ego state is called the parent. It is developed simultaneously with the child ego state and psychologically records a number of rules, regulations, and behavior patterns that judge actions and govern behavior. The third ego state is called the adult. This ego state processes information from the parent and the child ego states, as well as from itself, and deals with the reality of the moment. The adult ego state takes information given to it from the parent state to determine if the transaction is valid and true for that moment, and takes information given to it from the child state to determine if a particular feeling is appropriate in response to a transaction. The adult state comes to a decision using this information called "I'm OK-you're OK" or some other combination, such as "I'm OK-you're not OK," and so on.

Steps for implementation can be illustrated as follows. "I" messages are used by a parent to identify and define a problem for the child, such as "I've been very upset lately because you've been coming home too late from school. I worry so much about you, I can't get anything done." Possible solutions are generated when the parent says something like, "What can we do to solve this?" Solutions are elicited at this point from the child, and both parent and child evaluate them. The child, for example, may suggest, "Well, I suppose I could keep better track of time. If you would get me a watch, I'd know when to stop playing and come home." If this solution is acceptable, the parent might respond by saying, "Let's try it out to see if this will work." The next step involves determining if the solution has worked and if improvements need to be made in the compromise.

The advantages of this technique include:

1. placing part of the responsibility for conflict resolution with the child;

2. encouraging the development of a child's cognitive skills in suggesting solutions;

3. increasing communications that leave nondestructive emotional effects on both parent and child;

4. eliminating the parent's need to express power; and

5. encouraging autonomous behavior from the child

This strategy is significant in recognizing the influence of children's behavior on that of parents and in showing how to teach children to recognize the rights and needs of parents. Perhaps even more importantly, the strategy provides ways for parents to interact equitably with children instead of relying on power-assertive methods that damage children's self-concepts. Gordon recognized that there are times when active listening "I" messages, or the "no-lose" methods are inappropriate, such as when a child's safety is endangered; however, the methods are generally good and useful.

When individuals interact, the ego states of both persons are involved. Communication proceeds efficiently under a variety of circumstances, but it is especially efficient when transactions between ego states of individuals are parallel or complementary.

Transactional analysis (TA) is applied to parent-child relations by emphasizing the parent's analysis of transactions between himself and the child and determining which transactions were inappropriate. Most conflicts, from the TA point of view, are produced when the parent makes an adult-state request and receives a child-or-parent state response from the child. This provokes a child-state response from the adult, and causes effective communication to cease. TA encourages the parent to consistently develop his adult-state so that the child can have an appropriate model for developing his own adult ego state. This level of interaction teaches the child appropriate methods of behavior because children develop their adult states from models presented by parents. By emphasizing what parents can achieve through non-judgmental adult-state responses, TA seeks to alter parent-child relations so that children's behavior will change in the process. When children learn the vocabulary of TA, it becomes possible for them to point out to parents, as well as to themselves, when someone is not using his adult ego state in interpersonal interaction.

TA emphasizes the importance of "strokes" in maintaining good communications with others and in building one's self-confidence. Physically, strokes are touching others in a nurturant, positive manner. Psychologically, strokes are a recognition of others by interaction with them. Strokes can be either positive or negative and can be either conditional or unconditional types of social reinforcement. For example, when someone says to another, "I like you a lot," this statement is an unconditional positive stroke. Similarly, when someone makes the statement, "I'll spank you if you don't do as I ask," the person is making a conditional negative stroke in interpersonal interaction. The position of TA theory is that people need to determine the types of strokes they need from others. Children learn to expect these strokes in interactions with parents.

Ginott's Humanistic Strategy

Haim Ginott's text, *Between Parent and Child* (1965), represents one of the early contemporary strategies aimed at improving communications between parents and children. Ginott's philosophy of parent-child relations focuses on the avoidance of conflicts by showing parents how to listen to children and how to get children's full attention. Parents are also shown how to look for the "hidden meanings" of children's communications. Ginott's strategy educates parents how to take a therapeutic or counselor role with children and how to communicate their feelings to their children.

Communications with children are based on respect and skill. Parents are advised not to attack or criticize a child's personality or character but to focus on the offensive behavior. Parents are taught to look for the reasons that children misbehave. A typical Ginott-type response would be, "I'm angry and very irritated at what you've done; not at you." The adult is shown that he can help a child learn how to express his emotions, how to label these for future recognition, and how to react in the future in similar situations. Parents reinforce more positive self-concepts in their children if the behavior of the child is distinguished from the child who performs it.

Praise and positive reinforcement should not be overused by parents. When used, they should be directed toward reinforcing a child's *realistic* attempts and accomplishments.

A number of patterns of parent-child interaction are considered to be self-defeating. Threats are invitations for misbehavior because children are dared to repeat some forbidden act. Bribes gain only short-lived changes in children's behavior because they communicate doubt about a child's ability to change. Sarcastic comments only serve to make children feel bad about themselves, and children soon learn not to lisen to parents who moralize and preach about their faults and shortcomings.

Communication becomes more effective when physical differences between parents and children are minimized. One way to achieve this is by stooping or sitting down to be at the same eye level as the children.

Children can learn to assume responsibility for their own behavior by being offered acceptable alternatives to their behavior. Instead of asking, "What do you want to wear this morning?" Ginott suggests that parents should say, "Do you want to wear the blue pants or the green ones?"

Children learn discipline and responsibility through reasonable limits established by parents, limits that they can understand. Comments such as "Stop doing that" identify unacceptable acts but fail to guide children into acceptable behaviors. Alternatives should be given: "If you need to hit something, Tommy, use the sofa cushion, not your sister."

Physical punishment achieves less and is more damaging to a child than verbal communication. Children's misbehavior and conflicts are better managed by discussion of the problem. Physical punishment communicates the idea the "big people can hit little people without repercussions."

Ginott's approach to parent-child relations was accepted by a great many people because it recognizes a child's contributions to relations with parents as well as influencing the parents' behavior toward the child.

Driekurs' Democratic Child Training Strategy

Driekurs' theory (1958) represents a strategy of parenting based on a number of assumptions:

1. Behavior is purposive or caused; it does not merely happen.
2. It is necessary to understand behavior in its social context.

3. Goals of behavior explain actions.
4. To understand a child's behavior, one needs to understand the child's interpretation of the events he experiences.
5. Belonging to social groups is a basic need of people, both young and old.
6. People, including children, develop a life plan that guides their behavioral decisions even though these decisions may be based on faulty assumptions.

The starting point for developing an effective, loving relationship with a child is for the adult to learn the impact of the family unit in shaping a child's emerging patterns of behavior. The family is seen by Driekurs as the child's model for social interaction. The life plan— that is, the consistent pattern for decision making that guides behavior— is first encouraged and developed within the family. The life plan is based on decisions about behavior that relate to the ways goals are reached. It is a plan of behavior that a child discovers to be effective in solving particular problems. As children grow older, logic is developed to justify action constituting the life plan.

Driekurs believes that there are four types of misbehavior that occur from flaws in the logic of the life plan:

1. attention getting ("showing off" or crying) that is either positive or negative and makes others notice the child;

2. social power by doing what he or she wants and refusing to cooperate with others, which the child uses to control others;

3. revenge as antagonistic behavior, making others hate him by which a child makes a niche in a group; and

4. displaying inadequacy, in which failure in all endeavors is expected and is used by the child to escape participation with others

Driekurs' approach is well known for a particular method of child training that features teaching the child the logical consequences of his behavior. The democratic aspect of his philosophy emphasizes the equality of all family members in working together for the efficient functioning of the group. Social groups function well when the individuals understand and follow rules that govern the behavior of all, according to Driekurs. Parents and children are encouraged to discuss family rules and reasons underlying the rules. For example, a mother may wish to serve family meals at certain times and if someone arrives late for a meal, the logical consequence may be eating alone, eating cold food, or cleaning his own dishes.

When parents use logical consequences to teach the results of behavior, Driekurs believes that children quickly learn to control and take greater responsibility for their actions. The most difficult aspect of this method is for parents to enforce the logical consequences of the rules. It takes courage to allow a child to learn, sometimes quite harshly, the effects of his behavior on himself and on others. By experiencing the consequences of his behavior, a child learns to conform to expected standards to ensure the fair treatment of all family members. Parents encourage children to learn effective interpersonal interactions through methods like these.

No one strategy guarantees consistent results in its application to the parent role, but the four approaches have common characteristics, as summarized below:

1. Reduction of parental power. These strategies can be considered to be child-oriented methods of child-rearing that recognize the children's needs in relation to those of the parent. Power in itself is not seen by the advocates of these strategies as the cause of difficulties in parent-child interactions. The premise is that it is the way power is used by the parent that causes difficulties, and children are usually pictured as the victims of parental power. Power-assertive methods of controlling child behavior include physical punishment, such as spanking, and psychological punishment, as in shaming or making derogatory remarks about a child's character.

2. Improving children's self-control. These patterns focus on democratic interactions that attempt to teach children self-control as they progress through the more advanced levels of development. The parents transfer some portion of their power to the child by teaching him to take greater responsibility for his own actions.

3. Accentuating nurturance in caregiving. Each strategy attempts to accentuate the aspects of teaching and caring for children within the parental role. Several strategies encourage parents to adopt a counselor role by listening to children's problems in an understanding and helpful manner.

4. Understanding children's behavior. Most strategies teach parents the causes of children's behavior. Principles of child growth and development are included in the instructions parents are given for particular patterns of interaction. Parents are taught to recognize how differing levels of development cause differing problems and changes in children's needs.

Program Models

Family Service Association of America

In 1974, The Family Service Association of America appointed a national task force for Family Life Education, Development, and Enrichment. One of the goals of the task force was to assess the importance and future directions of the Family Life Education service with family service agencies. The agency provided a series of workshops organized around communication and self-concept objectives and step-by-step instructions for managing the parent group lectures, accompanied by handouts of practice exercises.

Education by TV Model

Parent Education by TV is a program that began as a joint effort between the Hawaii State Department of Education and a closed circuit television series. It was later developed for open circuit broadcasting to new parents in their homes. The major objective of the series, titled "Hand-in-Hand," was to enhance the development of self-esteem in parents and children. Emphasis was on self-worth, communication, flexible rules for family living, child learning, child care, and linking the family with society.

A Foster Care Model

The Early Childhood Program of Hanhemann Medical College and Hospital in Philadelphia, Pennsylvania, in collaboration with a large foster care agency in Philadelphia, developed an education model for foster parents of children who were one month to three years of age. The program goals for the foster parents are to expand their knowledge of normal child growth and development; to provide guidance on child rearing; to suggest ways to encourage children's intellectual, emotional, and social growth; and to provide a framework for development of a continuing education group program for the parents (Gross et. al., 1978). For further information on this model, write to Early Childhood Programs, 230 N. Broad Street, Mahnesmann Hospital and Medical Programs, Philadelphia, Pennsylvania.

A High School Model

The Children's Center is part of Princeton High School's child development course in which juniors and seniors are given the option to supplement their textual studies of child development by enrolling in a credit-based laboratory course involving the Children's Center day care programs. Four days a week, thirty preschoolers spend a half day, fifteen children in the morning and fifteen in the afternoon, at the Children's Center laboratory. During the term, the students log their activities and record their observations of how each child progresses in areas of physical coordination, for example, or the ability to solve puzzles.

Another high school program designed for "Anyone who has ever been a child" bases the curriculum on the different types of parenthood and the implications of each in terms of effects on the child. Also included are the common myths of being a parent, the developmental stages of children, the role of the parents from expectations and feelings to fears, the ways parent and other adult models for young children, sex education and sex roles, nurturing, and the different types of discipline and how to use them positively.

High schools are increasingly stabilizing the environment for both the single or married teenage parent and their children by providing relevant instruction. One high school offers an ongoing school year program which helps to decrease the number of school dropouts by allowing students to enter the program throughout the school year. After their babies are born, the students have the option of returning to their home school or finishing the school year in the Young Mothers Program. Students receive instruction in prenatal care, nutrition, postnatal care, and infant care before their babies are born. In the second part of the program, after the students return from the birth of their babies, the program concentrates on child development, family relations, role identification, health and safety, and specific problems with young children. The Young Mothers Program has developed into an excellent instructional program for pregnant teenagers and young mothers (Phillips and Baker, 1977).

An Urban Model

SUCCESS is a systematic program designed to help urban parents improve their effectiveness as educators and builders of self-esteem by helping their children to develop positive self-concepts. The SUCCESS program is based on two concepts: success, the achievement of predefined goals, plays a major role in determining a child's self-concept and future goal-setting behavior; and systematic parental attention and positive reinforcement are basic to helping a child feel successful and valuable as a person. The orientation sessions augment the parents's understanding that parents are primary contributors to their children's sense of worth. Following orientation, small workshops of ten to fifteen participants concentrate on role-playing and are programmed around three so-called "Action Phases" of rapport building, mutual goal setting, and success sharing.

Federal Government Models

Education for Parenthood originated in 1972 by the Office of Child Development and the Office of Education. The purpose of the program was to help teenage boys and girls become competent parents. State and local education agencies and community organizations also combined resources and talents to meet the objectives of the program.

Under one phase of the program, the Education Development Center of Cambridge, Massachusetts, developed a one-year elective course of students in grades seven through twelve. Curriculum materials include film strips, teacher and parent guides, and more than seventy information booklets. The materials concentrate on child growth and development, on skills in working with young children, and on the functioning of the family in society.

Another federal model, the Exploring Parenting Program, is designed to help parents increase their knowledge and skills in the following areas:

1. responding to children's needs and dealing with problems

2. observing behavior, looking for the reasons behind it, and understanding its effects on others

3. understanding the typical pattern of child development, individual differences, and the special needs of children with handicapping conditions

4. supporting and promoting children's development

5. clarifying values and teaching children to live by them

6. recognizing personal needs and finding ways to meet them

7. identifying sources of stress and forms of support.

Parents already possess most of these skills, but many are unaware of the degree to which they have and use these skills everyday or of the importance of these skills in supporting positive, healthy development in their children.

Exploring Parenting represents a unique approach to parent education in that the materials and the suggested instructional techniques recognize that there are many diverse styles of parenting, each founded on one's cultural background, personal value system, and the individual differences in both parents and children. It concedes that there is no one "right" way to parent. The program is built around the knowledge that parents already possess a wealth of experiences, knowledge, and skills; it addresses itself to the enhancement of existing competencies by using a variety of participatory activities. Specific address where additional information on the model can be obtained is Eduation for Parenthood, Curriculum Guide, Office of Human

Development Services, Administration of Children, Youth and Families, Children's Bureau, Publication (OHDS) 77-30125, U.S. Department of Health, Education, and Welfare, Washington, D.C. 20023.

Parents of Handicapped Children Model

Many parent involvement programs for the education of handicapped children stress the performance of the child rather than the performance of the parent, but the Portage Parent Program was designed just for parents. A Parental Behavior Inventory is conducted to assess the parents' strengths and weaknesses. The strategies used after these are determined are positive reinforcement, modeling, recording, and corrective feedback. The parents are given readings on major topics in teaching and child development. Home teachers are also used. Throughout the program, parents gradually assume more instructional planning and recording responsibilities.

The P. T. A. Model

The national Parent-Teacher Association (P.T.A.) is pushing hard to make parenthood education available through the public schools from kindergarten through twelfth grade. The members believe each community should develop a parenthood education program to reflect its own needs. The March of Dimes is also working with the P.T.A. is sponsoring national conferences on parenthood education. There have been sixteen conferences over the last five years, and as many as eighteen states have carried out projects for parenthood education (Baisinger, 1978). Additional information on this model may be obtained from PTA-Give Your Child A Good Start, National Congress of Parents and Teachers, 700 North Rush Street, Chicago, Illinois 60611.

The Expectant Parent Model

The Expectant Parent Program is a prevention program developed by volunteers in Bedfore County, rural area in Pennsylvania. Classes include the topics of conception, gestation, aspects of pregnancy, family planning, labor, delivery, post-delivery, post-natal care of mother and infant, characteristics of newborns, mother and infant nutrition, baby foods, principles of child development, development through play, and resources available through the county. The program was designed to reduce neonatal deaths, minimize medical problems of young children, allay expectant parent anxieties, and increase parenthood education. In evaluation, the program met its goals, satisfied the needs of the local community, and employed the information obtained from the parents, such as information on finances, toilet training, preparation of baby foods, role changes for fathers, and LaMaze childbirth classes.

The Fatherhood Project

The Fatherhood project is the first international effort to encourage new options for male involvement in childrearing through research, demonstration, and dissemination. One of the project's primary goals will be to facilitate networking among parents, professionals, and practitioners who share an interest in fatherhood. The project is currently assembling and operating a national clearinghouse on fatherhood, including information about programs and resources in the areas of employment, law, education, health, mental health, social services, and religion (Family Resource Coalition, 1982). For more information please contact Project Manager, The Fatherhood Project, Bank Street College of Education, 610 West 112th Street, New York, New York 10025.

Child Welfare League of America Parent Education Project Model

A national project to develop and demonstrate a parent education program for teenage mothers — and the more than half-million babies born to them each year — has been launched by the Child Welfare League of America.

The project is funded by a three-year grant totaling $482,247 from two Ford Foundation Urban Poverty Programs, "Child Survival/A Fair Start for Children" and "Welfare and Teenage Pregnancy."

In the project, which will be conducted at child welfare agencies in six cities, mothers, age thirteen to twenty, will attend weekly group meetings beginning in their last trimester of pregnancy and continuing for two years following the birth of the child. Topics of the weekly sessions will focus on child development, health care and nutrition, use of community resources, and the mothers' education, economic stability, goals and plans. Women of similar background and experience but who are older than the group members will serve as group facilitators and big-sister models.

The curriculum for the project is based on a peer self-help approach developed by Minnesota Early Learning Design (MELD). The Child Welfare League will work with MELD to adapt the curriculum for teenagers, oversee the groups, and evaluate the results.

Demonstration programs will be conducted in Cincinnati, Toledo, Chicago, Charlotte, Minneapolis/St. Paul, and Atlanta (Human Development News, 1983).

Additional information may be obtained from Shelby Miller, Project Director, Research Center, Child Welfare League of America, 67 Irving Place, New York, New York 10003.

Planning Content

Planning parent education programs is the responsibility of the director or the parent coordinator of a school or community organization, but the planning group should include parent representatives. Format and content should reflect the needs and interests of the parents and be adjusted to the level of education and previous training of the parent population. Programs that serve families from diverse education, cultural, and socioeconomic backgrounds should present a wide variety of choices from which the parents can select the programs that are best suited to their needs (Sciarra, 1979).

Issues of Content

There are four primary issues centering on content in parent education:

1. the efficiency of the format to be used,

2. a focus on prevention rather than therapy for childhood behavior problems,

3. teachable content for programs, and

4. concern that the mere provision of information may not produce changes in parent behavior (Dubanoski and Tanabe, 1980).

In regard to implementation of content there are two approaches: direct and indirect or, in other words, in person and in print.

Major Problem Area

Most parents seek parent education programs because of their feelings of inadequacy or the inappropriateness of their child management procedures. Disciplinary techniques are the major problem.

An angry child can be puzzling, draining, and distressing. One of the difficulties in confronting anger in children is that anger is often stimulated in the adult as well. Parents, teachers, counselors, and administrators need to remember that they may not have been taught to adjust to anger during their own childhood. For many, to be angry was to be bad, and one was made to feel guilty for expressing anger. In managing angry children, actions should be motivated by the need to protect and to teach, not by a desire to punish.

One should distinguish between anger and aggression. Anger is a temporary emotional state caused by frustration; aggression is often an attempt to hurt a person or to destroy property. Anger and aggression do not have to be negative terms. In looking at aggressive behavior in children, one must be careful to distinguish between behavior that indicates emotional problems and behavior that is normal.

Role of Discipline

Most parents do not understand the true meaning of discipline. They consider discipline to mean punishment. Discipline can be positive and include creating a quiet atmosphere of firmness, clarity, and conscientiousness while using reasoning. Bad discipline involves punishment which is unduly harsh and inappropriate, and it is often associated with verbal ridicule and attack on the child's integrity (Anderson, 1978). When a problem arises with children, adults often try to approach the problem with punishment. Authorities recognize that a positive approach to child care and development requires that the care giver distinguish between punishment and discipline in order to resolve the problems. Punishment usually stops the offending behavior but can have negative side effects. For example, the child may harbor resentments toward adults who are shown in aggressive acts or sneaking behaviors.

The generally accepted goal of positive discipline is to help children develop good self-concepts and healthy, functioning consciences. Positive discipline is challenging; it is sometimes hard work, but it is usually not as hard as the endless quarrels, power struggles, and rule-enforcement tactics that occur without it. It is sensible to take a solution-oriented approach and use diplomacy. However, sometimes words will not work and actions are called for, especially when there is a danger of physical harm or when a child is too upset to talk or listen. But when actions are necessary, it is important to remember that restraining a child is not physical punishment.

The most important element to remember in disciplining a child is to act rationally. If the parent acts rationally, then the child is likely to react rationally (Edwards, 1977). Consider the following reasonable approaches:

Practical Suggestions for Constructive Discipline

1. be consistent

2. be clear

3. administer in private

4. be fair and understanding

5. be flexible

6. diminish dependency

7. be authoritative

8. spend time with your child doing constructive activities

9. encourage family activities

10. attend to personal and marital needs

11. teach right from wrong

Play As a Solution to Problem Behavior

It is important for parents to realize that if a stimulating play environment is established, it will prevent much disruptive behavior from the child because it offers the child a natural, active outlet for energy.

Play is a universal phenomenon of humans. Spontaneity and structure are two elements found in all play activities. In play, one discovers how to live in a particular society and what conventions, morals, and mores that society expects. Moreover, in play, one learns how society functions and on what socio-religious principles society is based. The importance of play in human experience has been widely recognized as an integral and inseparable part of growth and development in early childhood. Play has long been perceived as an activity characteristic of humans and has often been associated with the realization of human potential. Playful activity is voluntary and free. It is more than a cure for boredom; it is essential to a young child's intellectual, social, and emotional growth. Play provides activities for the release of aggression and frustration. It is important because it expands the child's knowledge of real life situations; a child learns to solve problems he himself initiates. In most play, a child talks to adults, to objects, to himself, or to his peers. There is social interaction. Play becomes the medium for learning about one's self and one's group. The child learns the limits of his social environment, and he learns to cooperate in group settings. Children become less egocentric when they play because they exchange roles, share, and empathize with each other. When children move objects around in an environment or mobilize adults and peers, they feel they control themselves and their settings. Children begin to believe they are important when they show competence in the social and physical environments.

"Research supports the belief that there is a great need to develop a play ethic for the schools to complement the life and work values already found there." Parents need to establish the same environment for exploratory play. For instance, the more manipulations done with materials, i.e., play, the greater the learning potential and emotional outlet for children (McIntyre, 1977).

Play is serious business for children. From infancy until the child enters school, more hours are devoted to play than to any other activity. Within the fantasy world of play, children are free to create their own experiences and relationships. They have the opportunity to explore their imaginations while retaining full control in the environment.

Contributions of Play

1. Social skills: Play builds interpersonal relationships and adds to an understanding of society as a whole.

2. Language: Play encourages reflective thinking and communication, broadens vocabulary, and helps in labeling and reading.

3. Motor Skills: Through play, children learn bodily control, improved small and large motor coordination, and increased agility from physical activities.

4. Mathematical concepts: Play aids in the discovery of spatial relationships and abstract ideas.

5. Freedom of action: While playing, children can perform without fear of failure or ridicule.

6. Judgment: By playing with others, children learn the difference between right and wrong.

7. Sensory awareness.

8. Powers of concentration.

9. Self-esteem: Since play allows a child to create and control events, it greatly improves his confidence.

Effectiveness of Training

The parent education approach is useful because it has the potential to improve family relations and encourage positive behavior in children. Although these and other advantages are claimed by the various parent training programs, few studies have been conducted to assess whether or not the goals of each program have been attained. In fact, the main problem in parent education is that very little research has been done to evaluate the effectiveness of any given parent education program.

Application Activities

1. List ten ways parents might establish effective discipline in the home.

2. Describe the progression of motor development from one month to two years of age.

3. List the pros and cons of spanking. Describe at least five alternatives to spanking as a means of discipline.

4. Write a list of at least ten safety rules for children under age two years.

5. Observe three parents communicating with their children. Describe the communication patterns and list ways in which you feel that communication might be enhanced.

6. Make a poster describing and illustrating the appearance of a normal newborn infant. Show the poster to preschool-age children and describe their reactions to such a poster.

7. Compare two of the following parenting programs. Which of the two do you feel would be more effective? Why? What changes would you make to provide a more appropriate program for your community?
   A. Exploring Parenting
   B. Gordon's Parent Effectiveness Training
   C. Berne's Transactional Analysis Strategy
   D. Ginott's Humanistic Strategy
   E. Driekur's Democratic Child-Training Strategy

8. Form a parent discussion group. Identify common parenting strategies. Discuss aspects such as consistency, setting a role example, expressions of affection, and dealing with age/stage behaviors.

9. Describe our philosophy of parenting. Include developmental considera-

tions, views on discipline, the parent's role in education, and preparation for parenthood.

10. Explore methods of discipline with a group of parents of three to five year olds. What are common problems? What are common approaches? Is there a positive or negative approach to discipline? What type of approach seems most successful?

11. Develop a series of play activities appropriate for:
    A. Infancy
    • one to three months
    • four to six months
    • seven to nine months
    • ten to twelve months
    B. Toddler
    • twelve to eighteen months
    • eighteen to twenty months
    • twenty to twenty-four months

12. Visit a clinic for teenage mothers-to-be. Have several of these young women describe what they feel is the "average" baby— including appearance, appetite, sleep patterns, and crying. How do these descriptions differ from reality? What are the implications for education?

Bibliography

Anderson, L. 1978. The aggressive child. *Children Today*. Children's Bureau, ACYF DHEW, January-February, Publication # (ADM) 797 – 81.

Baisinger, G. 1978. Parenting: A national PTA concern. *Health Education*, 9: 16 – 17.

Beard, R. 1927. *Parent education*. Minneapolis. The University of Minnesota Press.

Bell, T.H. 1979. The child's right to have a trained parent. *Elementary School Guidance and Counseling*. 9: 271 – 173.

Berne, E. 1964. *Games people play; the psychology of human relationships*. New York: Groce Press.

Brim, O. 1959. *Education for child rearing*. New York: Russell Sage Foundation.

Driekurs, R. 1958. The challenge of parenthood. New York: Duell, Sloan and Pearce.

Dubanoski, R., and Tanabe, G. 1980. Parent education: A classroom program in social learning principles. *Family relations*, 29: 14 – 18.

Earhart, E. 1980. Parent education: A lifelong process. *Journal of Home Economics*, 72: 39 – 43.

Edwards, W., Jr. 1977. The remedy begins at home. *School and Community*.

Ginott, H. 1965. *Between parent and child*. New York: Macmillan and Company.

Gordon, T. 1970. *Parent effectiveness training*. New York: New American Library.

Graston, C. 1978. Parenting education at the new futures school. *Health education*, 9: 13 – 15.

Gross, B., Shuman, B., and Tracy, M. 1978. Using the one-way mirror to train foster parents in child development. *Child Welfare*, 57: 685 – 88.

Handorf, K. 1978. Managing your emotions in parenting. *Practical education for parenting*. The Ohio State University Extension Service, Bulletin 632–5, Spring.

Lavach, J. and Ries, R. 1978. Ages and stages: Child development revisited. *Social education*, 42: 374 – 377.

McIntyre, M. 1977. Exploratory play: Beginning the development of scientific concepts. *Science and Children*, 15: 38 – 39.

O'Connel, C. 1976. Helping parents with their children. *Today's Education*, 65: 43 – 44.

Phillips, D. and Baker, J. 1977. Parenthood education: Meeting the challenge. *Forecast for Home Economics*. 23: 76.

Romatowski, J. 1976. Helping adults nurture humaneness. *childhood Education*, 53: 27.

Sciarra, D. and Dorsey, A. 1979. *A child care center*. Boston: Houghton Mifflin Company.

Sciarra, D. and Dorsey, A. 1979. The Fatherhood Project. *Family Resource Coalition*. A North American Network of Family Support Programs, 2300 Green Bay Road, Evanston, Illinois, 60201, June 1982.

Sciarra, D. and Dorsey, A. 1979. Parent Education Project. *Human Development News*. U.S. Dept. of Health and Human Services, OHDS, 200 Independence Ave., S.W. Room 356-G, HHH Bldg., Washington, DC, 20201, Feb./Mar. 1983, p. 4.

Wilson, W. 1979. Parent Training: Some observations. *Academic Therapy*, 15· 45 – 51.

4. Parents As Educators

Generalization

The latest research in child development strongly proposes that a parent can provide young children with experiences in the forms of games and play activities that will greatly influence future intellectual ability. In the reverse, one could say that if certain experiences are not provided during the first years of life, the chances of reaching the intellectual potential could possibly be reduced (Gordon, 1970). To extend this concept to include social as well as cognitive skills, it is recognized that the early childhood years are important in the development of a stable foundation for these vital life functions. The knowledge base for this chapter is predicated on understanding trends and methodology of the process that occurs when the parent assumes the role of an educator. The abundance of infant stimulation curricula and program development materials attest to the significance of involving parents as educators per se.

Objectives

1. To present the rationale and long-term benefits for having parents serve as teachers of their own children

2. To explain the program trends that have occurred in the past decade and illustrate how the direction promotes parents as educators

3. To interpret data and significant variables of several model programs

4. To identify strategies useful to parents for teaching children

5. To emphasize the importance of reading and highlight the general and practical efforts parents can make to improve a child's process of learning to read

Trends

As a consequence of child development research, an awareness of the major role of the parent as an educator is emerging. Analyses of parent behavior and child development now suggest the need to develop a life time and space perspective on education which recognizes the major role of a parent as that of educator (Towns and Jones, 1979).

The parents' involvement in the education process is beneficial to the children. It could be suggested that children perform better in school when they perceive interest and involvement on the part of their parents. It has generally been shown that better parent-teacher rapport resulted in children's significantly increased levels of self-esteem, motivation to learn, improved academic attitudes, and higher levels of reading achievement. Conclusions are that parent involvement in the school process help children develop respect for school, individual, and property rights, as well as develop a better self-image that was beneficial to reading achievement.

Most parents are capable of raising competent children if they have the resources to train and teach the children. A mother's realization of her teaching role is directed by her own requirements and interests and ultimately, a mother is the decision-maker and the teacher of her child.

The history of education also suggests it would be advisable to recognize the role of parents in the education process. The initial thesis of education through life experience in the family and community was followed by the antithesis of academic education in the schools. As a result, the education professions and institutions often assumed a restricted classroom program as opposed to a more comprehensive "life time" and "life space" perspective of education. Child development studies imply that academic education will not solve the problems of low scholastic achievement among disadvantaged groups, again suggesting that a prudent approach to education is through the family and community in addition to the schools.

Increasing awareness of the role of the parent in the child's education is shown by an analysis of parent involvement in early education. Parent roles in the classroom education of children— assistants, facilitators, teacher aids, volunteers, policy makers, and partners in the operation of the school— are differentiated from the independent roles of parents as teachers of their own children. Education for children is a constant need, but school policies seem to underevaluate the importance of parents in the education process. A parent is a child's first teacher and the home is his first classroom; therefore, school officials should encourage the parent to be an effective, powerful influence on the child.

Effective Programs

In reviewing the characteristics of effective parent-as-educator programs, it was found that they have been rather prescriptive with clearly specified objectives. Activities have been carefully developed to realize objectives and have been implemented with considerable consistency and uniformity. This type of program has readily achieved a balance between prescriptiveness and personalization between a parent-child dyad. Effective programs seem to produce behavior changes in the child with regard to maternal teaching style and attitudes, childrens' intelligence, language development, and exploratory behavior. In relation to the types of parents who benefit from parent education programs which emphasize the parent's role as a teacher of the child, it was found that the participants were relatively better educated, were younger, had fewer children, and were more likely to have had a history of involvement in community affairs. Programs that incorporate consultation through groups facilitate the development of peer group support systems, increase the ability to use peer group support systems, and improve the ability to use peers as information resources and supports in maintaining new behaviors. On the other hand, programs that use individual consultations only provide a more personalized and individualized development directed toward more specific skills (Stevens, 1978).

An inner city school system in a major eastern city constructed a short-term program for parents based on a preventative model of education. The goal of the program was to help parents recognize that they were their children's first teacher and that parents were a valuable resource for both the child and the school. Schools can promote good relationships with parents through early intervention programs developed to train parents, usually mothers, by way of direct instruction in the home. It is an expensive way to deliver training, even though the training is clearly both a preventative and a compensatory model. Another cost factor is that parent effectiveness training courses require leaders who are specialists in group processes and many schools cannot afford to hire them (Towns and Jones, 1979).

The Project Head Start Model

One exploratory study using the Project Head Start model attempted to research the differences in maternal attitude following involvement in Project Head Start. First, the mothers were provided the services of a trained social worker. As a result of conversations with Project Head Start directors, four objectives in the area of school-home relations were developed:

1. to change parents' attitudes toward school personnel

2. to change parents' attitudes toward school policy

3. to change parents' attitudes toward readiness activities in the preschool curriculum and

4. to change parents' attitudes toward the way their children are treated by school personnel

Home Start

Home Start programs give parents, parent substitutes, and other appropriate family members an opportunity to learn the following:

1. various approaches to child rearing

2. ways of using elements of the child's typical environment as teaching tools, such as household articles, a television set, magazines, a grocery store, etc.

3. ways to turn everyday experiences into constructive learning experiences for the child

4. ways of encouraging the child's language development

5. ways to enhance the child's social and emotional development

6. various effects of the interaction between parents, children, and other family members

7. specific information about health and nutrition

8. resources in the community and ways of using them

The program must involve fathers, or father substitutes, whenever possible and it must make provisions for evening and weekend services to families. In recruiting, training, and supervising, Home Start staff must include trained paraprofessionals, parents, and volunteers. Parents are also encouraged to provide career development opportunities for staff; for example, training programs for Home Start staff should qualify for course credit in academic institutions whenever possible. Trained Head Start parents should be considered for Home Start staff positions and, through career development, they should be considered for Head Start staff positions.

Home-based objectives should aid parents in promoting their child's development. Parents should understand the objectives and consider them an important part of parent involvement. Home-based child development programs are created by parents who are trained in contemporary early childhood education and focus on:

1. the total development of the child

2. the competence of parents

3. the influence of family and home environment, and

4. early detection of developmental handicaps

The home-based teaching program practices essential principles of learning, such as:

1. learning should be problem-centered

2. learning should be experience-centered

3. experiences should be meaningful to the learner

4. experiences must be geared to the learner's needs

5. the learner must have feedback about the progress he is making toward his goals, and

6. the security of the learner must be protected

The objectives of the Home Start program are:

1. to enable parents to become more effective teachers of their preschool children

2. to facilitate the development of preschool children so they will be better prepared for successful classroom learning

3. to facilitate the integration of the preschool philosophy and format into the curriculum expectations and strategies employed by elementary school teachers

4. to increase communication and collaboration among school personnel and members of community institutions

5. to increase the community's understanding of, and encourage support for, preventative education which is aimed at helping families before children become excessively frustrated in the classroom or become school dropouts

6. to conduct research designed to improve the understanding of the learning process and identify the procedures needed to provide early environmental intervention

Home Visitors

Professional and paraprofessional home visitors can teach parents to guide their children in experiences which enhance cognitive development. Frequently, this guidance involves new ways of reacting to everyday events and new ways of using simple household materials available to most parents. Home visitors can also help parents discover ways of interacting with their children to improve social and emotional development. The intent of home learning programs is to help people discover how they can use their own parent potential to create a home environment that augments the child's total development. Studies show that home learning programs benefit the target child but also result in a beneficial diffusion effect to siblings. Some researchers believe this form of intervention may prove to be the most economical and effective way of reaching the greatest number of preschool children.

The Home Start demonstration program is one of the Office of Child Development's most visible signs of interest in supplementing family life and helping parents. Although evaluation studies are not complete and the Home Start program is comparatively new, two analyses have emerged:

1. many parents reflecting different ethnic and cultural backgrounds eagerly welcome home visitors and want to be part of a program that supports their own relationships with their children

2. paraprofessionals can be trained in a relatively short period of time to perform the complex and sensitive tasks associated with a home-based child development program

Other Home Learning Models

The "Learning to Learn" program in Jacksonville, Florida, teaches parents of preschoolers and first-graders about their children's curriculum, school behavior, and teacher-child interactions. The program encourages unguided home learning activities and has successfully improved academic achievement.

In Houston, Texas, school administrators developed a program called Operation Fail-Safe. Lists of suggested reading and simple home activities for parents and children were developed through the use of computers. When the project began in the fall of 1978, nearly three-quarters of the Houston parents with public school children attended the highly publicized individual conferences with teachers. During the conferences, the children's basic skills and achievement were discussed, along with ways parents could help promote reading ability.

The Project Home Base program in Yakima, Washington, also offers proof that children can be immeasurably helped during their first few years by their potentially best teachers, their parents. This Home Base program stresses conversations between parents and children and includes 200 individual tasks for children of various ages, each with a specific goal or aim. Parents are continually encouraged to adhere closely to a number of effective teaching techniques, such as eliciting questions from the learner, asking questions that have more than one correct answer, asking questions that require more than simple one-word answers, praising the learner when he answers well, urging the child to respond according to evidence rather than to guess, and allowing the child time to think out a problem before receiving assistance.

The Perry Preschool Project was an experimental program used to assess the long-term effect of a preschool program on the intellectual development of functionally retarded, culturally deprived, Negro children. The two-year program consisted of a daily three-hour class and a weekly ninety-minute home visit to the children in the nursery.

Home visits were conducted to achieve two objectives: to individualize instruction through a tutorial relationship with the student, and to make parents knowledgeable about the educative process so that, as part of their everyday lives, they could foster their children's cognitive growth. To achieve these objectives, mothers were encouraged to observe and participate in as many teaching activities as possible during the home visits. A weekly education program was conducted in the homes of disadvantaged preschoolers as a complement to a half-day nursery class. Mothers were involved in the educative process in varying degrees and maintained their interests over a two-year period, but the quality of participation did not improve after the first year. Physical conditions in the home created difficulties; especially troublesome were crowded conditions and poor illumination.

In the Perry Preschool Project, residence in public housing was found to be one of two variables related to relatively low growth in the intelligence quotient. The relationship was seen as possibly reflecting a lower level of aspiration among project residents and a resultant submersion in a low class population. The second significant home visit factor was participation by other children in the teaching session. This suggested that the most critical aspect of the home education program may not have been parent involvement but may have been the opportunity provided for a tutorial relationship between teacher and student. The ideal home visit program may combine both elements and consist of a private instructional session with teacher, mother, and preschooler participating (Radin and Weikart, 1966).

Chicago's Operation Higher Achievement involved students, parents, teachers, and principals, all of whom made contractual commitments. Parents promised to give their children wholesome food and appropriate clothing, to encourage their children by reading to them, and to insist that their children spend time studying. The students promised to strive to do their best every day. Teachers met with parents during special weekend workshops to discuss how to improve education; they visited the students' homes and often took special reading materials. Parents were encouraged to visit their children in class more often. The 400 children who participated in this program showed more than a six-month gain in reading achievement over children who were not involved.

A study conducted by the Wisconsin Research and Development Center for Cognitive Learning also involved contractual agreements. In this study the parents promised to hold reading conferences two times a week and to engage in a variety of activities related to reading, such as visiting the child's class, reading cooking recipes with the children, and going to the library with the children. The teacher's contract committed him to a meeting twice a week with each child, and to the preparation of a weekly progress report which was sent home to the parent. In this experiment, the children who had formed a learning partnership with their parents gained twelve months' achievement in reading scores, while a control group of children who did not participate in the experiment gained only one month's achievement.

The program labelled "Preschool Readiness Outreach Program," or PROP, was designed to share with parents of three-, four-, and five-year-old children ways they could help their children to develop beginning reading skills. Central to PROP was the belief that every child's life has activities which, with just a little planning, could be the beginning of reading-learning experiences; junk which, with just a little work, could be transformed into reading games; and parents who, with just a little PROP, could provide their children with experiences to extend their beginning reading skills. Weekly workshops and monthly pamphlets were used. The workshops consisted of twenty-six three-hour sessions weekly. The goal was for each parent to construct an educational game which could help his child develop a skill basic to beginning reading. Nine pamphlets suggested ways to use readily available activities to stimulate and extend children's beginning reading and language skills (Cassidy and Vukelich, 1978).

Assisted Reading Model

Parents are always involved in providing the linguistic environment in which their children learn to talk. Children learn to speak the language of their surroundings without formal training. Since not all parents provide their children with a rich linguistic and experiential background, children develop varying degrees of readiness for reading.

Teachers are sometimes unable to suggest simple means by which parents can assist their children. The techniques of assisted reading may be one way parents can become actively involved.

Assisted reading is based on the assumption that children process written language in a manner similar to the way they process spoken language. The similarities exist in the manner in which parents read to their children. Children who are listening to stories and are following the lines of print are essentially processing language that is more syntactically complete than some of the spoken language they hear. A child who follows the graphic stimulus with his eyes while being read to is in effect having an experience very similar to his first exposures to language. During his initial stage of exposure, the child organized the sound system, the syntax, and the semantic relationships of the oral language. In learning to speak, the child reconstructed the grammar of his particular speech community. He formulated the semantic relationships with his real world, the internal conceptual and lingusitic relations of his abstract world, the syntactic patterns of grammar, and the phonological rules by which he communicated his meaning through speech. In learning to read, the child must apply this knowledge to the printed word as he is reading, in much the same way he applies it while listening (Hoskisson, et al., 1974).

In focusing on some of the current issues in beginning reading instruction, emphasis has been placed on supportive home-school relations with recommendations for what can be done at home and at school to nurture successful children.

Reading is essential. It is fundamental, indispensable, and primary. Yet, as important as reading is, its role in a communications process is greatly influenced by the broad range of communication skills of which it is only one part. The abilities to listen, speak, and write are also essential to the well-being of children, and the development of these skills is closely intertwined with that of reading. Parents and teachers should concentrate on what they are doing to promote the language arts of listening, speaking, reading, and writing. Research indicates that children who do well in one area of language tend to do well in other areas.

The child's preschool years are critical to his development and preparation for school and for later life. The intellectual, emotional, and physical development that begins in infancy is reinforced or redirected during this time.

Value of Reading

Reading can be an important part of a child's life. A child's curiosity can be stimulated through reading and through discussion that usually follows. Reading is an excellent way to develop a child's language skills, as well. Through the use of children's books, the child's curiosity provides feedback to the mother, which has a positive impact upon the mother's thinking about her child.

Reading aloud to a child helps him expand his curiosity and helps foster a togetherness relationship between parent and child. It is not enough to surround a child with reading materials; he also needs the attention and positive attitudes of a significant adult. The parent should talk about word meanings, play reading games, talk about books that have been read or will be read, and read aloud to the children. The family who values reading will produce children who can read well. It is primarily up to the parents to see that their children become good readers (Weiser, 1974).

The most significant determinant in a child's reading development is the quality of his interaction with his parents and the nature of the home. A parent's reading habits are the main influence on the child. The home environment is a prominent factor in the child's attitude toward reading and in determining his reading success in school (O'Rourke, 1979). With the proper training, parents can function as their children's teachers. Researchers have reported that parents can effectively enhance their children's pre-reading and reading skills (Cassidy and Vukelich, 1978).

In a study conducted to determine when a child should begin to read, the University of Kanasas Child Development Laboratory concluded that reading might be a desirable curriculum option for children as young as three or four years old, provided they are ready to learn to read. The same study showed that "Children are never totally ready or unready to read. Reading readiness is nothing more than reading instruction in its early stages" (Goetz, 1979). If a child picks up a book placed among his toys, he may then be ready to read. If the child ignores the book, he may not be ready to read. Parents have to decide when their children will begin reading. One way for parents to decide which book is appropriate for the child's reading level is to have the child open the book in the middle, read the page, and count on his fingers each unknown or difficult word. As a rule, a book which contains more hard words than fingers on one or both hands may not be worthy of the effort (Indriscano, 1978).

Parents can help their children enjoy reading. One way to encourage a child to read is to let him have a library of his own so he can choose the books he wants to read even if they are too hard or too easy for him. The parents should also be a patient listener when the child wants to read aloud. Helping him with the tougher words and praising him for being able to read well gives encouragement. The parent should not tell the child he must read instead of doing other things because it will discourage him from enjoying reading. A child needs to be read to regularly by an adult who can be asked questions. The adult should serve as an interpreter between author, the illustrator, and the child's knowledge and experiences.

Adult Education and Parents

A major part of the responsibility for capitalizing on parent involvement in children's reading lies in adult education. Some of the parent training may have to be through elementary and secondary school personnel who, in turn, will require specific guidelines in adult education in order to work with parents. Teaching parents how to help their children's reading progress appears deceptively simple, but much more is involved in the parent-child relationship and interaction. For example, attitudes, timing, person-to-person communication, and a degree of patience are but a few of the relevant topics which need to be covered. Added to these are equally important adult education techniques which are necessary to keep participants motivated and interested and to help them be successful in what they are undertaking (Larrick, 1976).

Mothers learn quickly to reinforce their children's correct responses and to supply unknown words in a nonthreatening manner. Mothers expressed pleasure at being able to help their children so much with so little effort. The evidence for parent-as-educator involvement is made more compelling by the dramatic changes in the children's reading behavior. Previously, children had expressed dislike for reading and often had refused to cooperative in reading instruction. This study demonstrates that an economical, efficient, and effective program to help poor readers in primary classrooms can be easily established. The parents were quickly trained in the assisted reading technique and rapidly acquired the skills needed to reinforce their value judgment properly.

A helpful ten-point guide presented here will assist parents in preparing a proper and productive home learning atmosphere of older children. These guidelines are also recommended for professionals who help parents avoid creating an alienating obstacle between themselves and their children.

Guidelines

1. The home learning situation must be positive. Do not initiate a home teaching session to punish a child for performing poorly in school. Teaching sessions should only be held when the parents feel they can be of some value to their child's education. If parents feel that they cannot help the child, they should not get involved. Parents must be a positive force, not a neutral or negative force. Most important, a teaching environment must allow the child to succeed. The child must enjoy working with the parent. He should not be nagged, lectured, or made to feel unimportant. Do not punish the child/student.

2. Working with a child must be enjoyable for the parents. Parent should not feel compelled to work with the child out of frustration. Rather, they should be motivated by the feeling that they have something to offer. If the parents do not enjoy the encounter, it is not likely that the child will enjoy it either. A punishing environment should be avoided.

3. A teaching session should be kept short. Never work with your child until he or she is totally exhausted. The session should end on a positive note. If the child is pushed to the limit, he will eventually dislike the teaching situation. A full and active fifteen-minute session can be more productive than a long and boring one-hour session.

4. Whenever possible, require the child to perform activities which can be observed and recorded because this will assure several outcomes. For one, it will require the child to participate actively in the learning. For another, it will provide an opportunity to judge the effectiveness of the teaching efforts. But most important, it will allow the child to witness improvements in learning.

5. Provide feedback for work well done. Frequent positive comments, such as "good job, right-on, and looking good" will encourage the student.

6. Use a quiet and comfortable work location. Distractions will hamper the session and should be minimized. Televisions, radios, stereos, siblings, or friends playing in or around the area will disrupt the learning environment. Also, a working area should be equipped with the necessary materials and supplies: a table top, desk, chair, good lighting, paper, pencils, crayons, rulers, etc.

7. Sessions should be planned for a time convenient to both you and your child. Avoid scheduling the work session when it conflicts with a favorite television show, playtime with a friend, other household responsibilities, or any other time which would require either participant to sacrifice. Late evening work, when both parent and child are tired, should also be avoided.

8. The learning task should be within the child's ability. The parents should remember that they are not totally responsible for the child's educational program since that responsibility also belongs to the school. However, their child's educational program can be supplemented by parental teaching efforts. While attempting to master limited skills, parents should be cautious not to overload.

9. Personalize the learning activity whenever possible. This may evoke a favorable attitude and response from the child. The more the activity relates to the interests of the child (e.g., sports, automobiles, models, fashions), the more the child will learn. The total teaching session may thus be more attractive to the child and result in greater achievement.

10. Present the child with situations in which he can apply new knowledge. This will help him retain what has been learned. The application of new information to a variety of new situations is one of the most practical ways to insure that the child retains the knowledge (Spadafore, 1979).

For very young children, a different set of guidelines or strategies must be incorporated. Young children are much less sophisticated developmentally than older children, and therefore they have a shorter attention span.

The Parent As a Teacher
Guidelines for Infants and Toddlers

Set some special time to encourage your child to imitate you. Arrange two to three minute intervals during which you and your baby can enjoy an activity together. You might do it as you are bathing or diapering the baby or you might rest a few minutes and give that time to the baby. Possible imitative behavior, depending upon the age of your child, includes pat-a-cake, waving bye-bye, making sounds, saying words or phrases, banging two cubes together, and building a tower of cubes. Follow these procedures:

1. Make sure your child is not tired, hungry, or otherwise upset.

2. Make sure you have the child's attention.

3. Perform the behavior, or say the word, sound, or phrase yourself. Smile while you are doing these things.

4. If the child does not immediately respond, encourage him by repeating the word or performing the behavior again.

5. Sometimes it is necessary to help the child through unexpressive behaior.

6. When the child does imitate you, show how pleased you are by giving the child a hug, smiling at him, and saying something such as "Good girl" or "Good boy."

7. Even if the child only partially imitates you (for example, he says "Da" instead of "Daddy"), smile, hug him, and say something affectionate anyway, such as "What a good baby."

8. If the baby is still too young to imitate you, it is suggested that you can imitate him; for example, when the baby makes sounds, you can make the same sounds. This is one way to teach the baby to imitate you.

9. Do not force you child to imitate you. If the child is bored or uncooperative, stop the practice and try again another time.

10. Keep records of your practice session on Home Recording Form VI: How Children Learn by Imitation: The Parent As a Teacher-Model (American Red Cross — Parenting).

Training Parents As Teachers

A teacher is not someone who inevitably "knows the right answers," "instills knowledge," or even "motivates the child to learn." A teacher is someone who responds to the abilities, needs, and interests of the learner by providing real opportunities for learner-initiated activities which contribute to development. Put differently, a teacher does not struggle to motivate the child but tries to create a social and physical environment in which the child's intrinsic motivation is not frustrated. Effective teaching requires that the teacher have an adequate framework— some view or model of learning processes and the course of development— for interpreting the learner's behavior and for formulating coherent, appropriate responses. Thus conceived, the teaching role is identical for both nonprofessionals and professionals and can be portrayed through films, role playing, game playing, and workshops for making appropriate reading accessories. Additional periodic meetings would be beneficial so teachers can share experiences and discuss how to solve the problems they may have encountered in their work with parents.

Planning Workshops

The first step in planning for a successful "parents as educators" workshop is to make a checklist. Make sure the program is carefully worded and easy to complete. The program should provide useful information regarding parents' readiness to become partners in the educative process and their expectations regarding the activities designed to help them reach their goal.

The second step is to see that the parents' home and work schedules, travel restrictions, and conflicts in meeting other obligations are considered when specific plans are made. The limitations of distance and public transportation may require that car pools be arranged. In some circumstances, the dismissal schedule may need to be adjusted.

The third, and probably the most important step is for the instructor to create a warm and friendly approach (Indrisano, 1978).

There are six types of parent as educators programs. The first program is based on information about issues. In this program, the instructor moderates a panel discussion on an issue of particular interest. In this case, the interest is reading. It helps parents interact with their children. The second type of program is a learning games workshop. Here, the parents construct games using household items. A similar workshop is in the creative arts and involves art, music, and dramatic activities. The fourth type of workshop deals with books and magazines. This program suggests that small groups of parents read the same short children's book or magazine articles as their child. This

way, the parents follow their child's reading. Another program welcomed by
parents uses the media. Parents learn how to use the television, radio, and
daily newspaper more effectively. The last type of program deals with community interests. It serves as a guide to local places of interest, recreational
and educational facilities, and short trips.

The purpose of the first program, which is based on information, is to help
parents incorporate understanding, skills, and reinforcement when dealing
with their child. The beginning portion of the program consists of a ten-hour
experience intended to give parents more positive and effective ways to interact with their child. The remaining portion of the program shows them how
to be more responsive communicators with their child. This is done in two
two-hour sessions that help parents facilitate their child's oral language development (Peters and Stephenson, 1979). Once parents are able to understand
their child's use of language, they can improve their child's success in reading.

The learning games workshop concentrates on functional or survival
reading. This is defined as the ability to read street signs, recipes, labels,
applications, and contracts (Cassiday and Vukelich, 1978). The goals of this
program are for each parent to construct games to reinforce survival reading
skills in their youngsters. The program is for parents of children ages five to
seven. At each workshop, the leaders present three different games. Each
game is developed on two levels of difficulty, and the parents decide the level
appropriate for their child. To help the parent in the decision, a pretest is
forwarded to each registered parent prior to the workshop.

This workshop has been proven beneficial to both parents and children.
Parents were easily able to see the value of the activities they were construct-
ing and were not threatened by any lack of knowledge about the reading
process. Parents reported that children enjoyed the games and other activities;
they noted that their children were particularly thrilled then they were able to
read the words in "the real world" (Cassidy and Vukelich, 1970).

The type of program that incorporates creative arts is featured in the
Instructor magazine, "Hip Pocket Reading Games" (McWhorter and Walker,
1977). This program is for children's use in the summer to reinforce the
skills they are taught during the school year. Ten areas in which the parent
can help the child are looking and listening, following directions, likenesses
and differences, left to right, top to bottom, the alphabet, letter sounds, sight
words, building vocabulary, comprehension, and travel games. A page in
each child's handbook is geared toward his particular needs. An example of
an idea presented in looking and listening is "fill in." The parent reads a

simple story, leaving out words that would be easy to fill in. The parent waits for the child to fill in the missing word. The program does not have to be returned at the beginning of the new school year. This program is just one type of reinforcement in the creative arts area. It is not required of the parents, but is beneficial to the child.

The fourth type of program integrates books and magazines. An example of this program is one sent by schools to parents with children enrolled in school, parents of newborns, and parents who have just moved into the district. It recommends that the parent read to the child fifteeen minutes a day, five days a week, for nine weeks. From this, a warmth and closeness develops between the parent and the child. Certificates can be awarded to parents who successfully complete the program, and an appreciation assembly may be held to personally hand out the certificates. The program also contains some sample activity sheets which are sent home to parents once 'a month. A monthly activity sheet is a reminder to parents so the program will not lose attention (Applegate and Schlegel, 1979). The program is rewarding for public and school relationship and parent-child relationship.

The fifth program involved media. A program of this type is promoted by the Electric Company. As part of the program's early development, the advisors of the Children's Television Workshop designated poor readers seven to ten years old as the most needy audience for the program. These were children who had already tasted failure in school reading programs and children for whom television could provide a nonthreatening, familiar alternative to the classroom experience. The focus of Electric Company is on the most basic reading skills, which is felt to be simple decoding skills such as the mastery of letter and sound correspondence. Consultation with experts in appropriate fields such as reading, language, child development, and educational research began as soon as the program was conceived, and they continued to play an important role throughout the years. The Electric Company program has been a well-received, successful education innovation (Children's Television Workshop).

The last program hinges on community interests and uses the school system concept of a field trip. This approach helps to reinforce reading skills and to encourage the transfer to reading skills to other areas of learning (Graef, 1978). Activities in decoding skills, vocabulary development, comprehension skills, and oral language and listening skills can be arranged for all field trip activities. The instructor can then compare the similarities of a field trip and a story using elements like characters, plots, theme, vocabulary, and specific sequential events. The child thus experiences how to transfer learning from one area to another.

A parent should represent the model of a lifelong reader whom the children will want to imitate. Parents can share the delight in reading not only by reporting on what has been read but by doing some of the reading during a time set aside for that purpose. The parent should become knowledgeable about children's literature in order to provide appropriate materials which will enable children to find personal value in reading. The parent can also provide opportunities for children to use reading as a means to help others.

Parents can help a child excell by using life's everyday resources to realize his goals. A parent can have a child list one goal to be pursued through reading each month.

To maintain control over problems, parents should take time for silence and reflection. This way the parent and child, with the help of the school, can enhance reading development.

Application Activities

1. Using household items, create developmentally appropriate "toys" for infants up to six months of age.

2. Survey ten children under age five:
   A. How many know and recognize the alphabet?
   B. How many are beginning to read a few words?
   C. Describe three activities that parents might use to enhance early reading skills and language development.

3. Interview two elementary school teachers. List ways in which these teachers have involved parents in their classrooms.

4. Develop a list of questions relative to parents' relationship with teaching their own children. Administer the questionnaire with a minimum of ten parents.

5. Make a home visit, taking with you a home teaching activity to share with parent/child.

6. Develop a case study report of how a parent teaches her child a particular concept.

7. Observe at least three mothers caring for their infants (birth to twelve

months old). Describe the language each mother uses with her infant.
Are these language patterns conducive to language development? Identify
why you feel these patterns are or are not conducive. Develop ten activities that would enhance language development in infancy.

8. Meet with a first grade teacher in your community. Identify children in
   her classroom who are having difficulty with reading. Develop home
   activities using the parent as teacher to enhance reading skills.

9. Develop a set of parent-teaching guidelines. Distribute them to local
   principals and guidance counselors. Obtain feedback regarding attitudes
   toward parents as teachers, the involvement of parents in educational
   design and planning, and the home versus school as the major educational provider.

10. Critique five models of "parents" programs. Finalize a set of generaliza-
    tions common to all programs. Further, identify those aspects which
    appear to be problematic.

11. Interview an elementary school principal about his perceptions and sug-
    gestions for ways in which parents can be integrated with the educational
    system.

12. Organize a group of parents (minimum of ten) and assist them in
    developing a parent-assisted reading program in their school district.

13. Develop a Home Training packet for one specific developmental level
    and conduct it with at least one parent/child dyad.

Bibliography

Applegate, S. and Schlegel, W. 1979. *Parents in reading· Administrators guide.* ERIC Documents 172 186, pp. 1 – 24.

Cassidy, J. and Vukelich, C. 1978. Surivival reading for parents and kids: A parent education program. *The Reading Teacher*, 31: 638 – 41.

Children's Television Workshop. 1978. *Children's television workshop.* The Electric Company, Final Report on a Television Reading Series, ERIC Document 162 639, p. 6.

Goetz, E.M. 1979. Early reading: A developmental approach. *Young Children*, 34: 4 – 10.

Gordon, I.J. 1970. *Baby learning through baby play.* A parents guide for the first two years. New York: St. Martin's Press.

Graef, A. 1978. Using fieldtrips to reinforce reading skills. ERIC Document 159 615, p. 4.

Hoskisson, K., Sherman, T. and Smith, L. 1974. Assisted reading and parent involvement. *The Reading Teacher*, 27: 710 – 14.

Indrisano, R. 1978. Reading workshops for parents. *Instructor*, 88: 98.

Larrick, N. 1976. From "hands off" to "parents we need you." *Childhood Education*, 52: 134 – 37.

McWhorter, K. and Walker, A. 1977. Hip pocket reading games. *Instructor*, 86: 42 – 52.

O'Rourke, W.J. 1978. Are parents an influence on adolescent reading habits? *Journal of Reading*, 22: 340 – 43.

Peters, N.A., and Stephenson, W.J., Jr. 1979. Parents as parents in a program for children with oral language and reading disabilities. *Teaching Exceptional Children*, 12: 64 – 65.

Radin, N., and Weikart, D. 1966. A home teaching program for disadvantaged preschool children. Ypsilanti, MI: Ypsilanti Public Schools.

Spadafore, G. 1979. A guide for the parent as tutor. *The Exceptional Parent*, 9: E17 – E18.

Stevens, J.H., Jr. 1978. Parent education programs. What determines effectiveness? *Young Childnre*, 33: 59 – 65.

Towns, K., and Jones, B.T. 1979. The ignored untrained teachers: Parents. Paper presented at the Annual Meeting of the American Educational Research Associaton, San Francisco, CA, April, 1979, pp. 1 – 19.

Weikart, D., and Lambie, D. 1968. Preschool intervention through a home teaching project. Paper presented at the 1968 convention of the American Educational Research Association, Ypsilanti Public Schools, Ypsilanti, MI.

Weiser, M.G. 1974. Parental responsibility in the teaching of reading. *Young Children*, 29: 225 – 30.

5. Parents and Community Support Systems

Generalization

Communities often lack understanding of or are complacent about systems that serve young children and their families. Misunderstanding and lack of support stem from an unfamiliarity with the needs of dysfunctional children and families, ignorance about provision of such services to these recipients, apprehension about the philosophy of support programs, and mistrust of the availability of quality programming and care. Attitudes and resulting actions of the local citizenry are important to the development of local resources.

People need help to learn how to live comfortably with their own families. Problems often appear to involve inadequacy in problem-solving techniques to change conventional patterns of behavior. Pressures on families to adjust to change have created needs for community support systems that include education in family living. Social service agencies have traditionally been multifunction family and children agencies with goals that strengthen family life through individual and family therapy (Levin, 1975).

Within the past century, society has recognized certain responsibilities to its children. This has been indicated in the development of public school education, child labor laws, and aid to dependent children. But the recognition that society must protect children from their parents or guardians is a relatively new development. If social service workers are important intervenors, they should be professionally obligated to stay informed.

Objectives

1. To develop a statement of rationalization for community support systems

2. To identify practical ways to design support systems

3. To review special community programs such as child abuse, safety, and nutrition and support system models that are most relevant to contemporary society

4. To explain evaluation and training systems which can be structured to promote comprehensive support for parents

5. To discuss new developments, major issues, and solutions relating to community support systems

6. To review and recommend program research identified from community support systems reviews and future forecasts

Attitudes Toward Use of Social Service

There is a general lack of awareness about the relevance and appropriateness of social services for children and families, and there is a possible distrust of some practitioners of social services.

In one study by Levin (1974), parents were asked, "If you should ever have a problem with your child, would you use the services of:

a school guidance counselor
a psychologist
a social worker
a psychiatrist?"

Fifteen to twenty percent of the mothers replied that they "would not" use the services of a psychiatrist, psychologist, or guidance counselor and about thirty percent of the mothers rejected the idea of a social worker altogether. There were variations of relations to social class status; for example, the lower her family income and level of education, the more likely the mother was to express willingness to use the services of a social worker, a clinic, or an agency. When the income and education level was higher, the likelihood was greater that the mother "would" take her children to a psychiatrist. Parents' spontaneous comments revealed their apprehensive, and sometimes hostile, attitudes.

But despite their apprehensions, there is evidence that parents will welcome a resource without hardship, fear, or humiliation if they can obtain help for their children (Lurie, 1974).

Parent Education— Worker Characteristics

Working with parents is a demanding job. It requires workers who are themselves exceptionally sensitive to other human beings, who can accept hostility and rejection without being devastated by it and without feeling the need to retaliate. It also requires workers who can share themselves without sharing their problems and who can befriend while maintaining awareness of their helping role. Workers must be able to think first about the parents' needs and not their own, and they should have a sense of self-worth and achievement that will sustain them through work that is demanding and brings few immediate rewards

Some communities are using interagency committees or multidisciplinary teams to keep track of cases, making decisions on diagnosis, treatment, and final disposition. Teams also provide interdisciplinary education for their members and can serve to educate the community as well. On-the-job support can be provided from conventional supervisions and staff meetings where workers describe their cases, discuss their feelings about them, and seek advice through staff get-togethers where newer techniques of role-playing, validation exercises, and facilitating are used to raise levels of consciousness (Davoren, 1975).

Reporting Agencies

According to Nagi, (1975) protective example agencies maintained that they "always" or "often" received reports from police departments. The second highest reporting was from public health departments, followed by hospitals. Schools had the lowest levels of reporting. All agency respondents reported that the most serious deficiency was in counseling services. The need for home support, placement facilities, and financial support were also frequently indicated. Related impediments to program effectiveness were lack of interagency coordination and inadequate qualified staff.

The Major Problem

The major problem with community support systems as they now exist is fragmentation. Families often experience disorganization because they must make contacts with a variety of specialized agencies. Each of the agencies has a specific function that meets just one specific need or provides one specific type of assistance.

This single-service approach has been the model developed through historical processes, and it reflects particular disciplines and territorial concepts. What is needed, however, is a multiagency or multidisciplinary approach. Although programs may use different methods to deliver services, such as center-based or home-based methods, the types of services offered within a program usually are not tailored to the specific needs of individual children or families. The net result is that some children and families may receive few services and others may receive services they do not need.

General Planning Features

Three broad processes of program development must be addressed: planning, development, and implementation.

Planning. Important activities include:

1. Organizing. The program staff must organize itself for planning, developing, and implementing the effort.

2. Recognizing a need or problem. Once an organization has been formed, the group must pinpoint the communication problem.

3. Researching. What are the demographics of the community? What leadership exists? What about socioeconomic levels? Ethnicity? How are the particular programs perceived in the community? How credible is the program? What local customs, history, and traditions have import for the communication activities? Does the program compete with others? If so, what are the implications of this competition?

4. Setting goals and objectives.

5. Identifying audiences. Be sure that efforts are directed where they will count.

6. Developing messages. What is it that should be imparted to the community?

7. Deciding on a method for delivering the message. Examples are media and person-to-person approaches.

8. Evaluation. Evaluating the success of the community efforts must be planned. Seek indicators that will tell of success or a positive impact.

9. Planning logistics include: who is to work on and coordinate the communication effort; what are the agency's protocols with the community; what other programs, if any, will this interface with; how much money is avail-

able; what type of talent (staff or parent group) can help in implementation; and what needs to be purchased?

Development. Once the initial planning has occurred, a local program can develop its communication efforts, including:

1. refining purposes, audiences, and messages in relation to the need

2. developing a theme for the overall communication endeavor

3. designing, developing, and acquiring media materials

4. designing and developing person-to-person, media, and public relation strategies

5. establishing an evaluation scheme

6. getting agency approvals as necessary

7. setting time-lines and responsibilities

Implementation. The local program can now begin to carry out its activities, which include:

1. distributing media materials

2. holding person-to-person events

3. gathering ongoing evaluation information

4. reviewing the progress of the communication efforts and making modifications as necessary

Multidisciplinary Approach

Graduate and professional schools do not often encourage the multidisciplinary approach in the delivery of services, nor do they assist in the preparation of professionals who can treat the whole problem with a multidisciplinary or team outlook. Current theoretical and practical techniques try to improve the prevention and treatment services that confront vulnerable families. The growth of teams, councils, task forces, coalitions, consortiums, committees, networks, and forums is not an accident but flows from the neccesity of support for families who are in need. A team concept can help mobilize services and support decisions, as well as uphold federal and other specialized standards.

Functions

Social Service systems within communities perform many functions, both direct and indirect services. According to Melvin, (1979) the functions are best carried out in teams and the organization for this are:

1. Indirect Service: Resource Networking

2. Direct Service: Case Staffing/Case Consultation

3. Indirect Service: Planning/Development/Evaluation of Services

Each one of these team groups contributes to a community's accepted responsibility for the prevention and treatment of family violence. Any one of these functions can be a community's starting point in developing an integrated system. Any particular team can blend various functions. Whatever the blend or developmental pattern and whatever the mix of teams and functions, the product is a network of services that strengthens families.

Staffing Systems

One measure of program quality is the training and commitment of its staff. Effective intervention builds on an institutional team effort involving a child care worker, a social worker, a teacher, a consulting psychiatrist, and a psychologist who all work closely together. A fragmented system cannot be tolerated. The team approach can be useful when team members respect each other and are flexible. Traditionally, the "helping services" worker is a family systems specialist and the child care worker is the prime caretaker of the child's physical and emotional needs. However, the interdisciplinary team must work out its differences and learn from each member. Some tasks may be accomplished separately; many tasks will best be accomplished together. The social worker, for example, should be physically located in the unit where the clients live in order to promote a level of trust (Finkelstein, 1980).

The challenge we face is not to discover what works, since we already know to a great extent what works, but to discover how to develop the cooperative community structures necessary to provide the needed services effectively and compassionately.

Federal Leadership

The federal Office of Human Development should lead in developing and implementing a national policy that clearly states areas of common interest in all family problems. The policy should promote noncategorical family-community service programs. The programs should specifically address the interrelationships of problems and emphasize the family stress model, as compared with the victim-perpetrator model, and promote networking for support systems. Other components which should be encouraged are more training and information, screening, referral, case management, and multi-disciplinary case conferencing (Washburn 1979 – 80).

A Model of Integration

In recent years, the federal Office of Child Development has initiated several research and demonstration projects which have produced significant findings on the delivery of integrated services to children and their families. Each of these programs, along with Project Head Start, uses a specific approach to the delivery of services. The purpose of each is to provide an integrated delivery of comprehensive services to children and families on an individualized basis. It is expected that such systems can be replicated in whole or in part by other child development programs, or they can create links between existing child and family centered service systems.

Two of the model integration programs are the national Project Head Start Child and Family Resource Program (CFRP) and the Parent-Child Center.

The CFRP attempts to provide an array of development services for low income families. It builds upon the multidisciplinary foundation of the Head Start child development concept, but expands the scope of the project to include children who are preschool and school age. The CFRP demonstrates a new dimension in the integration of child development services. It provides a system which will serve the needs of children longitudinally throughout the major stages of early development and provide appropriate services to parents and other family members in an effort to improve the child's development.

Principal objectives of the CFRP model are:

1. to individualize programs and services to the needs of children and their families

2. to integrate resources in the community so that families may choose from a variety of programs and services while relating primarily to a single resource center for all children in the same family

3. to provide continuity among the resources that are available to parents, enabling each family to guide the development of continuing through the early school years

4. to build upon the strengths of the individual family as a child rearing
   system that has distinct values, a culture, and aspirations. The CFRP will
   attempt to reinforce these strengths, treating each individual as a whole
   and treating the family as a unit

The Head Start experimental Parent-Child Center (PCC) program has
contributed significantly to a knowledge of the benefits of a continuous developmental program for a child's first three years of life. The PCC, Head
Start, and Home Start programs emphasize the role of the parent as a
significant prime influence in the child's development. School linkages assist
children and parents to make smooth transitions into school, supporting both
home and school efforts to minimize the potential of each individual child
and provide resources for the continuation of developmental services to families. The CRFP attempts to overcome the dramatic fade of developmental
gains that children may experience after they leave Head Start. (Melvin,
1979)

Other Comprehensive Models

A Child Welfare Model. Family Outreach was created by parents in con-
junction with other councils and departments. The center began with combined
community populations of 100,000 and school populations of about 48,000
students. It was staffed by a full-time caseworker and sixteen volunteers
trained as paraprofessionals.

Information, referral, and one-to-one counseling services were offered by
telephone and visitation on a continuing basis. Volunteers answered telephone
calls and counseled clients under the guidance of the Family Outreach caseworker. Volunteers were involved in all phases of the program, including
planning and fund raising.

The goals of the program are threefold: inform the public about child
abuse and neglect and reinforce an awareness of the community's responsibility; work for the prevention of child abuse and neglect by developing one-
to-one relationships with potential child abusers; find foster homes and adop-
tive homes in the community for the children.

March of Dimes — Birth Defects Model. The National March of Dimes
seeks to prevent birth defects through its support of:

1. a nationwide network of Medical Service Programs in genetic counseling,
   prenatal care, intensive care of the newborn, and exemplary treatment for
   children who are born less than perfect

2. basic research by outstanding scientific investigators who explore the causes and means of preventing birth defects
3. a comprehensive program of education for health professionals in the latest advances in birth defects prevention
4. broad-scale public education to increase the awareness of effective measure to prevent birth defects

Child Abuse Model. The Mayor's Task Force on Child Abuse and Neglect of the City of Detroit was organized in 1963 out of a common concern to coordinate agencies and work together on problems of child abuse and neglect. It encompasses a broad cross-section of organizations and professionals who meet once a month to engage in problem-solving tasks to achieve a more efficient utilization of the resources available. This task force on Child Abuse and Neglect is not a direct service provider; rather, it serves as the network through which all major child abuse and neglect concerns and programs are channeled.

The Task Force is credited with the leadership, planning, and direction of obtaining government funding for a one-year demonstration project which was the first interagency, multidisciplinary project on child abuse and neglect, the Child/Family Center. (Belden, 1979)

The Parents Anonymous Model. Parents Anonymous, Inc. of Los Angeles, California, is a private organization of self-help groups that now has 1,500 members in 150 chapters in the United States and Canada. The organization has programs planned for state departments of social services and other agencies that are involved in the problems of child abuse and neglect, as well as delegates to child welfare conferences, research advocates, and advisory groups. The organization, first known as Mothers Anonymous, was established in 1970.

In 1974, Parents Anonymous received a grant from the Children's Bureau, Office of Child Development, to help establish additional chapters by preparing and distributing materials about the organization and by providing technical assistance to communities that want to form similar groups, including the training of regional coordinators and local group leaders (Powell, 1979).

The Community Model of Industrial Day Care. Faced with lost hours of work due to absenteeism, tardiness, and high turnover rates, many employers are beginning to recognize that inadequate child-care alternatives can substantially affect company operations. Now that fifty percent of all children under the age of eighteen have working mothers, child care has become even more important. In order to recruit and retain employees, industry is going to have to be concerned about the need for child care. There are a variety of ways employers can help.

Advantages of an on-site center include closer family ties, quicker access in case of illness or emergencies, and on-going parental exposure to a child's development. The center has access to corporate resources such as medical services, computer time, typing services, and services of legal, personnel, and financial divisions.

Located away from company premises, the off-site center is usually community-based and operated by one or more employers, government bodies, and parents.

Consumer Supports for Children

Pressure from various consumer advocacy groups is creating improvements in the health and welfare of children.

Car Safety

The importance of having children travel in car safety restraints was verified by a recent study conducted by the Washington, D. C., based Insurance Institute for Highway Safety. A study of 26,971 revealed that unrestrained children in the front seat have the highest injury rate. Back seat location reduced the injury rate for unrestrained children; however, the restrained children had lower injury rates in both seating locations. Solutions for car safety appear to be as follows:

1. Young children, especially infants, should use specially designed child or infant restraint systems as a highly recommended first choice.

2. Lap belt restraints appear to offer protection even for younger children in the isolated crashes reported. Where child restraints are not available, parents should use a lap belt as a second choice.

3. Evidence overwhelmingly demonstrates that an occupant, whether infant, child or adult, is less likely to be killed or injured in a crash if restrained.

4. Child seats that hook over regular automobile seats should not be used.

5. Under no circumstances should any motor vehicle occupants, including children and infants, be unrestrained.

Project Childsafe is one of the major health education efforts of the Wisconsin Hospital Associaton Auxiliaries during 1975 and is endorsed by the Women's Auxiliary to the State Medical Society of Wisconsin, The Wisconsin Association of Women Highway Safety Leaders, Inc., and the Wisconsin Jaycettes. The purpose of Project Childsafe is two-fold:

1. to encourage parents to use proper crash-tested child restraints for all children under forty pounds or five years of age when riding in an automobile (models recommended are dynamically tested by the University of Michigan Highway Safety Research Institute)

2. to warn consumers that not all restraints are crash-tested and safe

The ultimate goal of Project Childsafe is to reduce the number of children killed and injured while passengers in automobiles. Increasingly, states are requiring the use of restraints for all young children. (Richardson, 1983).

Toys and Safety

Skates, tricycles, toy trucks, cars, nonflying airplanes, boats, toy wagons, and balls are among children's favorite play things. Last year, according to U.S. Consumer Product Safety Commission estimates, approximately 150,000 people received hospital emergency room treatment for injuries associated with toys.

Falls are the most frequent types of accidents, but many serious injuries result from children swallowing small parts or placing tiny toys in their noses and ears. Serious injuries also result from exploding gas-powered toys, from flammable products, and from objects with sharp edges.

The Commission has authority under the Federal Hazardous Substances Act, as amended, to ban hazardous toys and other children's products from sale. Since 1970, more than 1,500 items, mostly toys, have been banned. Despite the efforts of toy manufacturers, retailers, CPSC inspectors, Consumer Deputies, and other government agencies, it is impossible to examine all toys. It is possible, however, for parents, relatives, and older sisters and brothers to check every new toy purchased and every old toy around the house for possible hazards.

Do not buy or accept any toy that you cannot thoroughly inspect. Watch out for:

A. Plastic rattles, toys, instruments:
- can break easily
- sharp edges
- small objects

B. Wood toys:
- splinters
- lead paint

C. Squeeze toys:

- squeaker removes

D. Party toys:

- sharp wires
- sharp edges
- loose squawkers

E. Larger child's toys:

- sharp edges
- splinters
- weapon-like objects

F. Baby teethers:

- liquid or gel may be contaminated
- small objects

G. Stuffed Toys

- pins
- eyes that remove
- wires inside
- staples
- is it washable?

H. Dolls

- pins
- staples, buttons
- flammable hair and clothing

I. Electric toys

- sharp edges
- make sure all parts have been tested

J. Others that can hurt

- chemistry sets
- darts, bows and arrows
- BB guns, slingshots
- projectiles

Television As Support System

While television is not usually thought of as a support system, it has readily become such to American families. Research has shown that children three to five years of age average fifty-four hours of television viewing time each week. The average prekindergarten child spends more than sixty-four percent of his or her waking time in front of a television set.

A limited number of quality television shows have been designed for children, including such standards as "Captain Kangaroo," "Sesame Street," and the newer "Zoom," "Over Seven" and "After School Specials." Consequently, even the youngest children spend the great bulk of their television-viewing time watching inappropriate adult shows. Children who watch a lot of television can be characterized as:

- having a shorter attention span.

- thriving on noise, strife, and confusion.

- getting little sleep.

- having little respect for adults, including teachers and parents.

- regarding school as irrelevant or as society's sentence imposed on them.

- filled with hostility and prone to settling things by violence.

- having anti-interpersonal relations values.

- having anti-cooperation values.

- having anti-democratic values. (Larrick, 1975)

However, research in the past three years indicates that a more effective control of television's influence on children can be exerted from within the home. Citizens and consumers can influence the content of television. They can express their opinions and write letters about programs or commercials to local television stations, citizens groups, and advertisers. Letters can have considerable impact on stations and advertisers because representatives of those institutions realize that each person who bothers to write represents many more people with the same opinion.

Whatever action is taken, it should be remembered that television is a socializing influence on a par with family, school, and peer groups. How television is used in a home merits thoughtful attention (Huston-Stein 1979). The following are some specific strategies that can be helpful in giving parental guidance in the use of television in the home:

1. Talk with your child about programs that:
   - delight your child

   - upset your child

   - show differences between make believe and real life

   - show television characters who can solve problems without violence

   - illustrate how some things seen on TV hurts people

   - show foods that can cause cavities

   - show toys that may break too soon

2. Make your child aware of:
   - the number of programs that can be watched

- turning the set off when the program is over
- use of public television

3. Look at TV with your child for:

- TV behavior your child might imitate
- TV characters who care about others
- women who are competent in a variety of jobs
- people from a variety of cultural and ethnic groups

4. Substitute other appropriate activities such as:

- talk with each other or tell stories
- read a book, draw a picture, or play a game

Supplemented Food Programs

WIC is a government program that gives food to eligible pregnant or nursing women, infants, and children under five years of age. For infants (from birth to one year) who are bottle-fed, WIC provides infant formula fortified with iron. It also provides baby cereal and fruit juice. For mothers who are pregnant or are nursing, WIC provides milk (or cheese), cereal, fruit juices, and eggs so that basic body health can be maintained and breast milk will be good for the nursing baby.

WIC also gives milk, cereal, fruit juices, and eggs for children who are not yet in school. Growing bodies need proteins, carbohydrates, fats, vitamins, and minerals, and WIC foods have these important nutrients. The baby formula and the cereal have iron for healthy red blood. The fruit juice has vitamin C to help fight off infecton and heal wounds. The milk has calcium and vitamin D for strong bones and teeth. Eggs have a lot of protein which is used to build muscles and other parts of the body.

Integrated Support Systems

According to May (1977), positive elements of integrated support systems could be:

1. working relationships with other health agencies and professionals that have been improved through the creation of new mechanisms for information sharing

2. a new network of relationships that has been established with public library systems and medical libraries

3. the availability of a wide range of resources that have resulted in upgrading the caliber of community education programs and concurrently enabled agencies to become involved in additional educational efforts

4. inservice education and training programs that have been strengthened, by encouraging staff to keep informed of developments in the field and by having ready access to the most current literature

5. extensive statewide programs for the training of professionals that have utilized consultants and others with regard to training content and design

6. resource centers or research facilities that are available for students and serious investigators

7. agencies that are willing to experiment with new approaches to treatment

8. documentation of effective programs and evaluation of new programs as implemented

9. increased quality and quantity, local, regional, and national public relations efforts in the form of accurate documentaries, movies, newspaper and magazine articles, and public speakers

10. more public education about human relationships, beginning in preschool, day care centers, and elementary schools. This should include communication skills, how to verbalize feelings, how to express feelings in appropriate behavior, and how to negotiate mutually satisfying joint outcomes in their relationships

Concepts which can ensure success in program development efforts are:

1. solidify support for the communication effort within the program staff and agency before going public

2. collaborate with other local programs

3. build community awareness as a long-term proposition; goals concerning awareness and instruction may be accomplished sooner than goals concerning attitudes

4. identify and use people with credibility in communications efforts. They can serve as spokespersons or chairpersons

5. communicate simply, honestly and concisely, with sensitivity to audiences. Be positive in your approach, and prompt in delivering services. Be creative

6. be straightforward in approaching controversial topics or issues

7. strive for active participation and avoid passivity wherever and whenever possible

8. blend techniques for reaching some goals and audiences, i.e., mix radio, television and person-to-person approaches. Most persuasion happens as a result of multiple means

Specific parental needs within any community support system are:

1. someone who will be there with practical help in times of crisis

2. someone who understands how hard it is for parents to have dependents when they have not been so sure about what it is to be dependent themselves

3. someone who will not criticize them

4. someone who will help them understand their children

5. someone who can give to them without making them feel of lesser value because of their needs. Parents need to feel valuable, and eventually they need to be able to help themselves and to have some role in helping others

6. parents need help to feel good about themselves (Davoren, 1975)

Need for Research

Utilization of social indicators of the quality of life for families and children is a valuable tool with which to formulate questions and thus better focus attention and resources on families in need. The limited conceptual and empirical nature of child and family support systems may be augmented by a research-based experimental intervention model. The ecological approach presented here has scientific value in its contribution to child development and social support systems.

The ecologist's theoretical use of mapping as an essential tool in social analysis systematically studies the community context of parent-child relations and builds upon the compelling insight that while the child is father to the man the community is parent to the family, and, in so doing, it enhances an understanding of the ecology of human development (Garbarino and Crouter, 1978).

From an ethical viewpoint, family life and human services workers must continue to help the public accept the beliefs that are the foundation of child protective services: the dignity of the child and the child's right to good care and relationships with parents; the right of parents to fulfill their parental role; the desire of most parents to be good parents; parental neglect as an indicator of stress or disturbance; the capacity of people to change; and society's responsibility for children.

The task is enormous but a pragmatic approach will probably have a greater effect at this point. It is necessary to influence public opinion and legislators' opinions on a practical basis (Koerin, 1980).

In any case, discussions growing out of these contacts may lead to some change in emphasis, or a different balance among elements. As a participant in these discussions, the professional is a part of the ongoing process to accommodate the sometimes conflicting qualities of realism and idealism in the same statement. In this process, professional goals are entirely compatible with those of the self-help leaders (Powell, 1979).

Evaluating Community Support Programs

Efforts committed to the system is worthwhile if there is a plan to evaluate the effects from the first day the idea is discussed. The evaluation design does not have to be elaborate, but without a carefully planned design it will be impossible to make decisions about continuing the effort or improving the quality of the program or system. Some basic considerations are:

1. numbers of parents who indicated initial interest

2. number of parents who attended group meetings or, if they missed the meetings, contacted a staff member individually

3. quantity of printed handouts on activities and materials that were picked up by parents

4. number of parents who offered verbal or written comments about using activity ideas or kits

5. frequency of parent involvement in the program such as talking to the classroom teacher about the child's progress in the center or school

6. number of parents who filled in the progress charts and reviewed attainment of goals with staff

7. comments the parents made about how they perceived themselves as participants

8. differences that were observed in the behavior of children whose parents were involved in the program (trying new tasks, persisting, asking questions, expressing self freely, showing independence, self-starting, etc.)

9. the number of parents who volunteered to become actively involved

Regardless of the result of the evaluation, give formal recognition to all parents who committed time and participated in the program. One effective technique is to combine the recognition ceremonies with a social event, such as a coffee clatch or a community supper. Certificates of accomplishments might be awarded to the parents and teachers who have worked toward and achieved goals. For those who wish to continue, this might be a good time to cooperatively develop new goals for the coming year and to consider other strategies and activities. Acknowledge weaknesses, talk about all of the ideas that did not work, and review new approaches.

Application Activities

1. Interview three children (below age twelve) about their favorite TV programs. Are these programs generally desirable or undesirable?
2. Visit a toy department or store. Make a list of toys that would be safe for:
   A. an infant (0 – 6 months)
   B. a toddler (1 – 2 years)
   C. a small child (3 – 5 years)
3. Interview a parent about toy safety. Include aspects such as how toys are selected, how toys are maintained, what toys are generally safe or unsafe, and what toys do the parent's child/children enjoy most.
4. Observe infants and children riding in automobiles. For a minimum of ten observations, list the number of children who were: 1. properly restrained, 2. partially restrained, and 3. unrestrained.

5. Make an antidote chart for poisonous substances commonly found in the home. Include the local poison-control telephone number.
6. Analyze two TV programs intended for viewing by children. Compare and contrast the programs according to the standards applied to TV programs in general as well as those standards specific to children's programs.
7. Meet with a group of parents. Discuss methods to control the TV programs viewed by children.
8. Form a parent discussion group focusing on the topic of nutrition in infancy and early childhood. Subtopics might include: "Problem eaters," "Food allergies," "recipes children enjoy" and "providing a balanced diet for toddlers."
9. Write a parents' guide to toy purchase and safety.
10. Interview a representative of Parents Anonymous. Discuss such aspects of child abuse as incidence of parent/child need in the community, and risk factors, as well as methods of dealing in a comprehensive way with special parents.
11. Interview two different human services program directors using the criteria for program development outline in Chapter 5.

Bibliography

Belden, A. 1979. Mayor's task force on child abuse and neglect. *Midwest Parent-Child Review,* 4: 4, 1 – 12.

Davoren, E. 1975. Working with advisee parents, a social workers' view. *Children Today,* 4: 38 – 43.

Finkelstein, N.E. 1980. Family centered group care. *Child Welfare,* 59: 33 – 40.

Garbarino, J., and Crouter, AS. 1978. Defining the community context for parent-child relations: The correlates of child maltreatment. *Child Development,* 49: 604 – 16.

Huston-Stein, A. 1979. Children and television: effects of the medium, its content, and its form. *Journal of Research and Development in Education,* 13: 20 – 31.

Koerin, B. 1980. Child abuse and neglect; changing policies and perspective. *Child Welfare,* 59: 542 – 50.

Larrick, N. 1975. Children of television. *Teacher,* 93: 75 – 77.

Levin, E. 1974. Development of a family life education program in a community social service agency. *The Family Coordinator,* 24: 343 – 49.

Lurie, O. 1974. Parental Attitudes Towards Children's Problems and Toward Use of Mental Health Services: Socioeconomic Differences. *American Journal of Orthopsychiatry,* 1: 44, 109 – 119.

May, S. 1977. They said it couldn't be done— but it could. *Midwest Parent-Child Review,* 2: 1 – 12.

Melvin, M. 1979. Community networks. *Midwest parent-child review.* An interdisciplinary HEW, Region V, information exchange, 4: 4, 1 – 12.

Nagi, S.Z. 1975. Child abuse and neglect programs: A national overview. *Children Today,* 4: 13 – 17.

Powell, T.J. 1979. Interpreting parents anonymous as a source of help of those with child abuse problems. *Child Welfare,* 58: 105 – 13.

Richardson, Barbara. 1983. How To Choose and Use a Child Restraint. *Motor Travel.* Vol. 3: 1, 14.

Washburn, C.K., and Bell, T.R. 1978. Family violence: The issue today. *Midwest Parent-Child Review,* 3: 1 – 3.

Washburn, C.K., (ed). 1979 – 80. Child abuse and neglect and substance abuse: The wrong spread connection. *Midwest Parent-Child Review,* 5: 1 –10.

Washburn, C.K., 1967. Food Before Six. *National Dairy Council.* 6500 Rosemont, Chicago, Illinois, 60606.

6. Advocacy, Policy, and Volunteer Parent Involvement

Generalization

There appears to be strong support for the general principle of "parent involvement" or "citizen participation," and the idea can be translated into workable programs and structures that will impact positively for families, schools, and related social service agencies. Educators who want parent involvement look for meaningful ways to collaborate with parents to provide the best possible conditions for educating and caring for children. There is relevance in the variety of ways parents and teachers have collaborated in early childhood education— ways that may be useful to fellow professionals (Guttman, 1978).

Parent involvement in the volunteer, advocacy, or policy-making process for children can help to create a society in which having children is valuable, honorable, and enjoyable. Very specifically, it may be a partial solution to the lack of professional help, increase parental satisfaction with the school, carry educational principles into the home, reduce financial cost of education, provide insight into behavior of children, and help parents and teacher develop more rewarding relationships with children.

Granowsky et al. (1977) correctly state that "It is time to set goals and design strategies to bring this about." By setting specific goals and involving parents to the greatest degree possible, parents and community members will realize a program better able to reduce powerlessness and increase parents' influence to meet social, physical, intellectual, and emotional needs of children and other family members.

Objectives

1. To establish the general knowledge base for the consideration of parent involvement in advocacy, volunteer, and policy-making activities

2. To discuss the relationship between school officials and parents and, in so doing, establish the rationale for parent involvement in the school

3. To establish general systems of advocacy movements for parents, children, and families

4. To outline methods and strategies which will encourage parent leadership development

5. To recognize the importance of parents as volunteers and to explore a system for organizing parents as volunteers

Parent/Citizen Power

The governance of the schools must be shared among all the participants in the education process, including parents. Increasingly, parents, citizens, and organizations in which they participate are beginning to recognize that they are a force. This force is being translated into action, and school systems are reaching for parents and citizens and their organizations as powerful allies in the quest for quality schooling for all children.

Parents and citizens are joining the other three "forces" in public education — administrators, teachers, and school board members and their respective organizations — to share in the decisions which affect public schooling. The power of parents expands tremendously when an organized body of parents gathers to influence the school systems and the legislators. They feel changes must come about if the children they represent are going to get a "fair shake" in the current education system (Kappelman and Ackerman, 1977).

In a thorough study of early intervention programs, it is concluded that active involvement of the parents of children enrolled in the programs is critical to the program's success (Guttman, 1978). However, the success of parent involvement in decisions will largely depend upon teachers participating *successfully* (Marburger, 1980).

Many parents are afraid to go to the schools, and they feel uncomfortable when they do. School staffs should not let this happen; rather, they should go to parents and let them know they are needed. The core of the movement is made up of those parents groups who understand simply that parents are a special population in the school community. They have a unique understanding of what is best for their children, and they have a common sense right to strive for the best services for their tax money.

Laws Requiring Parent Involvement

A number of laws or legally binding regulations require parent involvement in the public schools. For example, Title I of the Elementary and Secondary Education Act of 1965 includes laws that provide states with billions of dollars for special services to low-income and educationally disadvantaged students. Title I requires Parent Advisory Councils for each school and each district with Title I programs.

Local School Advisory Councils are required for individual schools that fund vocational education programs under the 1963 Vocational Education Act. Parents of handicapped children must participate in every step along the way toward individual education plans for their children, according to the Education for All Handicapped Children Act of 1975.

The School Lunch Program requires parent and student involvement in menu planning, enhancement of the eating environment, program promotion, and related student-community support activities. Also, if a state agency finds a school has poor managment practices that hurt the real program quality, parents and students must be involved in developing, implementing, and monitoring a system to improve the situation.

Do not assume, however, that federal regulations automatically give parents the kind of basic policy-making and decision-making powers they deserve. The author suggests that most of these programs stress membership requirements and committee composition. They are often detailed and prescriptive on membership and very vague and general in regard to functions and conditions of operation. This is one area in which the professional parent-educator needs to expend more effort in translating "theory into action."

Volunteer-Advocacy-Policy Model Programs

There are numerous and varied models which are representative of those parent involvement, advocacy, and policy-making situations. Some of these are exemplary, such as:

1. Action Volunteer Programs

   a. Retired Senior Volunteer Program (RSVP) which has up to 101,612 members.
   b. VISTA. As of June, 1964, there were 443 VISTA projects in the U.S. involving 4,327 volunteers.
   c. University Year for Action. Fifty-five projects have been established with 1,715 volunteers.
   d. Foster Grandparents. 12,193 seniors are involved in this national program.
   e. ACTION grants to states. During the past two years, 23 states have obtained ACTION grants, and added governor-appointed State Offices of Volunteers to help coordinate and facilitate voluntary efforts at the state level. Some new organizations developed in the last decade are:

   The Association of Volunteer Bureaus
   American Association of Volunteer Service Coordinators
   American Society of Directors of Volunteer Services of The American Hospital Association
   Association of Voluntary Action Scholars
   International Association for Volunteer Education
   National School Volunteer Program

2. National Center for Voluntary Action (NCVA)

   Over 200 Voluntary Action Centers have been established across the country during the past three years.

3. Court Programs

   Many juvenile and adult courts in the United States now have organized volunteer programs (Bladley, 1981).

4. Parents Without Partners, Inc. (PWP, Inc.)

   An international, non-profit, non-sectarian educational organization devoted to the welfare and interest of single parents and their children. Its program and activities are entirely the volunteer work of members of PWP, Inc. (The Toledo Connection, 1979).

5. Parent Cooperatives

   These groups organize and establish policies for respective child development centers. At best they give creative answers to some of the deepest problems of our time. These are usually small, face-to-face groups that have a closeness, intimacy, and concern for one another comparable to that of large families in earlier days.

6. Head Start

The goal of the parent involvement component is to promote the growth and development of parents by having them assume an active role in every aspect of the program. (Pearlman and Williams, 1980). Generally a parent working on the policy council learns about alternatives and consequences (Coughlin, 1977).

With regard to volunteer, advocacy, and policy matters, Head Start mandates that parents:

a. receive preference for employment as a center paraprofessionl or non-professional. Parents may often serve in positions as classroom aides, nutrition aides, office workers, etc.

b. visit the center to see and observe how their children work and play with other children

c. volunteer to assist in the classroom

d. work with staff in planning activities for the children, and assist in preparing materials for classroom projects

e. become active members of the Head Start Center policy committee.

f. share program information with other parents

g. support and assist the Policy Committee and Council representatives — or serve as representatives

h. help to plan education programs of interest to themselves and other parents. Head Start staff and consultants have many resources available for this purpose.

i. work with other parents to help to resolve community problems in areas such as housing, health, and education

j. work in planning and carrying out fund raising activities

k. assist in developing and carrying out parent-sponsored activities that utilize Head Start parent activity funds

l. use home visit materials and ideas from center activities in working with children at home

m. share with Head Start staff their own suggestions and ideas for center learning experiences (Parent Handbook, 1980).

7. Title I Parent Involvement

Under Title I, each local education agency must describe how parents of the children are to be served. Parents should be consulted and involved in planning of the project, and should set forth the specific plans for continuing involvement in the future planning and in the development and operation of the project. Parents are included as observers or learners, as participants in school activities, as volunteers in the classroom, and as participants on school advisory committees. The types of activities conducted, the amount of parent involvement, and the effects of such involvement are examined. (Nebgen, 1979)

8. PTA (Parent Teacher Association)

Originally this assocation's relationship to schools was non-political in that their by-laws stated that chapters should "cooperate with schools. . . in ways that will not interfere with the administration." Delegates at the 1972 convention, however, replaced that clause with one that states that "local units should seek to participate in the decision-making process establishing school policy."

This change created a whole new ball game in the parent/citizen/school participation process, one that was necessary if PTA's are to serve their school's needs in the fullest and fairest way possible. What this change means to the PTA — and increasingly to administrators — is sharing in the decision making that directly affects children's education, being partners in the truest sense.

What is wanted is the opportunity for parents to bring their own informed opinions into an open discussion on school policies, programs, finances, and curricula with administrators and to participate in making decisions on these matters. (Sparling, 1970)

The National Parent/Teacher Association has recently advised that more parent advisory councils should be organized because such councils are "successful in implementing recommendations."

9. Buckley Amendment

Perhaps the most important educational reform of the 1970's was the Family Educational Rights and Privacy Act of 1974. Popularly known as the Buckley Amendment, it guarantees parents the right to see all official school records involving their children and limits access to these records by outsiders without parent permission. (Marburger, 1980)

10. National Center for Child Advocacy

In the spring of 1971, the United States Department of Health, Education, and Welfare (HEW), through the Office of Child Development (OCD), assigned the mission of establishing a National Center for Child Advocacy. OCD and other federal agencies were funding experiments, demonstration programs, exploration projects, and research efforts under the general heading "child advocacy" — as were some private foundations and local funding sources. But is was also clear by then that whatever child advocacy was supposed to be, movement, field, or program component was neither defined nor understood. There is not basis for separating the old-with-a-new-name from the new and because the initiatives are widespread, but there was no central source of information.

11. The Day Care and Child Development Council of America (DCCDCA)

The Day Care and Child Development Council of America was founded in the mid-1960s. It is a membership organization of individuals, day care providers, and day care organizations. Most of its support comes from grants from the Ford Foundation. It has grown from a small amateur operation to a large and well recognized national organization. In the later 1960s and early 1970s, the organization campaigned and advocated for universal, publically-funded day care and other pressing issues such as minority rights. The DCCDCA holds seminars all over the United States, and they participate in contemporary progressive social welfare movements and fund-raising benefits.

12. The Coalition for Children and Youth (CCY)

This group was formed in 1972 and also is a membership organization. A key part of this organization is its cluster groups. These groups of smaller organizations within the larger one support legislation, influence the administration of programs, and improve citizen involvement. Under this unusual arrangement the cluster can lobby while the main organization cannot. Each cluster handles a different area: health and day care, early education and family, parenting and foster care, adoption and youth services, and juvenile justice.

13. The Children's Defense Fund (CDF)

This group was founded in 1973 to provide long-range and systematic advocacy on behalf of the nation's children. It is staffed with educators, psychologists, lawyers, researchers and data analysts, health experts, social workers, and writers. It works at federal, state, and local levels and chooses to reform indisputably harmful policies and practices affecting large numbers of children (Romanofsky, 1978).

In many ways, the leading child advocacy organizations founded within the past 20 years are growing up. They are beginning to stand on their own without financial support of charitable foundations and federal organizations. Their success or failure could have long-term significance for child welfare in general and federal legislation in particular.

Parent Policy Programs: The How and Why

The major variable associated with the development of policy are those that deal with character and importance. Policies provide guidelines for achieving program goals. If policies are inadequate or absent, the administrator hesitates to make decisions because he fears admonishment. This results in crisis-to-crisis operation and inconsistency in the decisions that are made. If policies are constant and apply equally to all, they assure fair treatment and provide a basis for evaluating existing plans and determining the merit of proposed plans. Policies should:

1. be written in keeping with the restrictions of law and regulatory agencies in order to be valid

2. cover all aspects of the local program or, at minimum, cover those situations occurring frequently

3. be developed for the various aspects of the program

4. be followed consistently, with exceptions stated in the policy

5. not be highly specific, as they are guidelines which establish the foundation for administrative consideration and action

6. be written and be readily available so that they can be interpreted with more consistency by those concerned

7. be relatively constant and not alter with changes in the membership of the board

8. be subject to review and modification since their validity rests on current state laws and regulations of other agencies

Policy categories could be:

1. Administrative: the procedures, organizational details, appointment, and functions of the director and board members

2. Staff Personnel: recruitment, selection and appointment, job descriptions and evaluation, tenure, separation, salaries, absences, and professional activities.

3. Recruitment: admissions, attendance, services, child's progress, and special activities.

4. Business: funding, budgets, expenditures, guides for purchasing, accounts, and auditing procedures.

5. Public Relations: type of public participation, use of facilities, media use, and relationships with other agencies.

6. Component and Areas of Specialization: education, social services, medical services, nutrition counseling, etc.

7. Training and Technical Assistance: inservice, credit-based education and other forms of education.

One of the policies could be to write a set of bylaws; a sample outline for bylaws follows:

Article 1:   Name of the policy group

Article 2:   Purpose

Article 3:   Goals or objectives

Article 4:   Meetings
  Section 1:   When will regular meetings be held?
  Section 2:   How can a special meeting be called if it is needed?

Article 5:   Membership
    Section 1:   Eligibility
    Section 2:   Selection of members
    Section 3:   Length of membership
    Section 4:   Voting rights of members
    Section 5:   Number of people needed to be present at a meeting for official business to be carried out (sometimes known as a quorum).

Article 6:   Officers
    Section I: Officers' titles, such as Chairperson, Secretary, Treasurer
    Section 2:   Election of officers
    Section 3:   Term of office
    Section 4:   Duties of officers.

Article 7:   Committees

It is helpful to have special committees which take on certain responsibilities such as personnel, finances, publicity, career development, and training.

Article 8:   Method for amending by-laws (Parents Handbook, 1980)

Volunteerism: Principles and Process

The following six principles are important in establishing and maintaining a good relationship with volunteers.

1. The most valuable resource in a voluntary service is the people who function within it.

2. People are motivated to join voluntary groups to accomplish a task and to satisfy socio-emotional needs.

3. Certain kinds of behaviors are required for volunteers to satisfy their task and socio-emotional needs.

4. Good staff relations and volunteer relations are crucial to the proper functioning of the service.

5. Approaches used in recruitment and orientation of volunteers must be compatible with the philosophy of the service.

6. Volunteers must be recognized with appropriate non-monetary rewards.

Increasingly, human service agencies are being held accountable for gifts of time, effort, money (tax or donation), materials, and the use of talents. Good management of volunteers is important and takes planning, preparation, organizing, and overseeing with constant concern for individuality. Recipients of the volunteer services are the most important people in the hierarchy. Volunteer managers must ensure that the recipients have good experiences and relationships with the volunteers who reinforce and extend use of the agency services. Promoting volunteerism increases possibilities for real social action and community change, new roles for older people, and career exploration for the young.

Most people have altruistic reasons for volunteering but others have a healthy streak of self-interest. Whatever its motivation, volunteering can mean self-renewal for both the volunteer and the community. Industry has found that the motivating factor keeping people on the job is the work itself. This is certainly true of volunteers as well. The volunteer coordinator should give structure, organization, and purpose to the volunteers. Volunteers should be included when decisions are made, should be made to feel a part of the organization, and should feel that they have an important role.

Designing Jobs and Recruitment

1. Do specific, rather than general, recruiting whenever possible.

2. Have a year-round recruitment plan.

3. Use a variety of recruitment techniques, for example, newspapers and displays.

4. Be sure to use the services of the Volunteer Bureau, the Voluntary Action Center, or the Retired Senior Volunteer Program.

5. Recruit by inviting people to respond to the opportunity to volunteer, not by telling them they ought to be concerned.

6. Be enthusiastic!

7. Opportunities to volunteer must be expanded to include all segments of the community.

The Volunteer Coordinator Role

The main responsibilities developed for the volunteer coordinator are keeping records, acting as liaison between the volunteers and teachers, recruiting parents and teachers, coordinating inservice and orientation programs, publicizing the programs, organizing volunteer recognition activities, and evaluating the program. This means the volunteer needs to know all jobs in the program and have the capacity to understand and recognize individual strengths and potential as each volunteer is assigned or placed in a particular role.

Besides being sincerely interested in the person, two of the most crucial interviewing skills are the ability to ask appropriate questions and the art of listening.

One of the most interesting, yet difficult, things about interviewing is that the interviewer must establish instant rapport with a person; this means the volunteer coordinator cannot have biases toward race, religion, cultural, or educational background. Interviewers must accept and be able to relate to all people.

Volunteers represent valuable time and energy resources. One of the best "how to" suggestions for effective management of volunteer programs includes:

At a center:

observing in the classroom

helping with art media

helping with music and rhythm activities

storytelling— giving undivided attention to a respective child

helping to prepare materials for creative activities

accompanying children on field trips

preparing a class scrapbook

helping with out-of-door free play or special activities

helping children brush teeth and wash hands

helping at meal time

accompanying children to dentist and doctor appointments

using the special talents of volunteers

assisting in woodworking

singing and playing an instrument

photographing important activities

assisting with field trips

addressing envelopes and letters

answering telephones

helping with the newsletter

typing

At home:

telephoning other parents for meetings

washing and sewing all doll clothes, costumes, etc.

preparing art materials

donating clothing

babysitting while parents attend meetings; observing in the classroom

repairing books, toys, and equipment

collecting and saving materials for use in the classroom

baking cookies for class parties

In the community:

help to recruit children for program

help to recruit and train other volunteers

help with public relations and special events

serve on program planning committees

serve on community committees

help at the Clothing Center

Advocacy: Components and Process

Advocacy is a planning, coordinating, and monitoring system to assert priorities on behalf of the constituent group. Advocacy can improve the provision of services if it is better conceptualized, given supportive structures, and allowed to focus more systematically on its unique methods and processes. Advocacy needs organizational support, but not overly tight bureaucratization. Advocacy should be promoted as a planned function yet permitted to flourish as a spontaneous cause. It is no substitute for resources, personnel, or sound general social policy. It always requires that someone cares or is strongly motivated by a sense of fairness or law.

Child advocacy appeared during such an era of social reform — the 1960s. The concept was attractive because it combined the promise of needed change with a lack of specificity; that is, it represented a kind of social venture and eventually was identified as an activity that might be financed. Child advocacy understandably took many forms and had many sponsors.

The Effective Parent Group

Whether the effort be related to policy, volunteering, or advising an effective group of parents and staff, the effective parent group must first of all be relaxed and comfortable. Each person should feel that his contribution to the group is important and that the members are interested in what he has to say. All members of the group should be able to help others feel wanted and important. Members should be aware of the knowledge they and other members possess which can be exchanged to improve the program. Group meetings should be such that all members feel encouraged to contribute ideas and suggestions and that these will be thoughtfully listened to by others in the groups. Each member of the group should not only contribute individual ideas but also encourage others to do the same. The group needs to be effective in carrying out the planning, policy-making, and decision-making tasks necessary to run the center.

One major goal of all effective leadership for parents is to tie every short-term victory to a long-range plan for policy change. Without long-range change, the same problems will surface time and time again, and new groups of parents will have to deal, each time, with the old problems. Only democratic leadership can assure steady progress toward long-range goals.

Just as a leader cannot be defined in terms of title or personality, so leadership cannot be defined in those terms. Leadership is not a person. Leadership is a quality, the ability to motivate, direct, and inspire others to reach group goals and satisfy group interests. Leadership is a series of actions or operations which help the group toward its desired ends. It is the art of bringing change about; it is a process that people use to reach their objectives and realize their goals (Della Dora, 1978). As related to parents, the author suggests that good leadership should be expected "for" and "from" parents.

Organizing a Parent's Group

The realization by parents that they have a problem but that they do not know how to solve it leads to consistent expressions of frustration.

An important beginning is to choose a name for the group. This brings ready identification in the community. The choice of a name should be a group decision, and the name itself should reflect the goals and special role of the group. It should be a short name that is easy to say, Existing groups, for example, call themselves Parents United, Parents' Union for Children, Advocates for Children, Our Kids, Parents for Better Schools, and Parents for Education.

Much depends on how receptive the school or agency and related officials are. It is advisable to inform school authorities or other agency managers that a parents' group is being formed. A few officials and parents should be invited to a planning meeting.

The meeting place should be a public building, if at all possible — a school, a community center clubhouse, or a library.

The group should not concern itself immediately with bylaws. This can sap energy that would be better channelled toward planning action, fact-finding, defining issues, and expanding membership. Agree on rules as the need arises instead of spending hours on the wording of bylaws. Once a comprehensive set of working rules has been established for elections, voting privileges, dues, meeting frequency, committee structures, and affiliation with other groups, legal steps should be taken to incorporate (Riouz, 1980). This will enable the group to file for state and federal tax-exempt status.

The next step is to develop a list of major concerns which will become the goals of the group. And finally, the group should be kept together. The work of advocating is never finished. There will be more to do, even if one day it consists of simply offering a support system for parents whose children are newly involved in educational services (Hoppe, 1979).

Parliamentary Procedure

Eventually, parents need to learn proper and acceptable organizational procedures. Parliamentary procedure for conducting meetings should be considered *mandatory* for training parents. This technique is fundamental and accepted by all professionally organized and recognized groups as the way to take orderly action. The ability to conduct business using a logical procedure allows parent groups to be more effective and cohesive in other processes for acquiring benefits or program needs. Preliminary to the actual technique of conducting meetings, the professional volunteer or parent coordinator should assist parent groups in looking at the process from a "total meeting view." A sample agenda is:

1. Call meeting to order

2. Roll call (optional)

3. Minutes of previous meeting

4. Reports of officers: president, vice-president, treasurer, secretary

5. Standing committee reports

6. Special committee reports

7. Unfinished business

8. Postponed business

9. New business

10. Adjournment   (Sponberg, 1948)

The coordinator will be the key person in training parents in precise parliamentary procedure and should obtain clear and easy to understand training materials for them. It would be wise to get the Robert's *Rules of Order* booklet, but described below is a sample of how to handle a motion:

1. Get recognition. Get the chairperson's permission to speak by saying, "Mr. (or Madam) Chairperson."

2. Make the motion. Offer your recommendation to the rest of the members by saying, "I move that we survey the number of unemployed heads of families in our neighborhood."

3. Second the motion. Another member must approve your suggestion before all of the members can consider it. To support your idea, another member should say, "I second the motion." Your motions cannot be discussed until it is seconded.

4. Clearly state the motion. The chairperson puts the motion in words that everybody can understand and then states it loud enough for everyone to hear: "It has been moved that. . ."

5. Discuss and restate the motion. The chairperson invites members who are for and against the motion to discuss it. Start the discussion by asking the person who made the suggestion to support it. A chairperson cannot offer his opinion on a motion unless he leaves the "chair" by having another officer take his place. The discussion ends when the chairperson prepares the members for voting by restating the motion.

6. Vote on the motion. The chairman reads a motion before calling for a
   vote and there are different ways to vote:
   Vote by written ballot. This method is used when voting in important
   matters. A motion that cannot be debated must be made before this
   procedure is followed. Two or more tellers are appointed by the chairman
   to conduct the vote. They distribute, collect and count the ballots. A
   written tabulation of the vote should go to the secretary and results are
   entered in the group's official record. A simple majority is needed to win
   a ballot vote.
   Vote by voice. The chairman first asks members if they favor a motion:
   "All those in favor of the motion say 'Yes'." And then, "All those against
   the motion say 'No.'"
   Instead of calling for a YES or a NO, the chairman may find it easier to
   use the words FOR or AGAINST, PRO or CON, AY or NAY, etc.
   Vote by a show of hands or standing up. The chairman asks all members
   in favor of the motion to raise their hands or stand. He then asks all those
   against the motion to do the same.
   Any member can question the results of these two voting methods by
   "Calling for a division." The chairman solves the problem by asking each
   member who favors the motion to please stand and be counted. He repeats
   the request for those opposing the motion.

7. The result. The chairperson announces whether or not the motion has
   been approved by reporting the outcome.

Officers and their usual duties are:
The Chairperson·

- keeps the meeting moving, keeps speakers on the subject.
- sees that members understand what is going on, which rules apply, and
  why.
- allows full discussion so that people are clear about the issues
- protects the minority. Allow someone to speak for the motion, then alter-
  nate with someone against it.
- serves as a moderator and only takes sides to vote in case of a tie. The
  position of chairperson should not be used to push a particular decision
  against the will of group members.

The Recording Secretary·

- takes minutes of the meeting and prepares them for presentation.

- helps the chairperson follow the agenda and write down and read the motions when they are needed.
- records all votes taken at the meeting and summarizes all reports briefly.

The Co-chairperson:

- substitutes for the chairperson when she/he is absent from the chair.
- assists the chairperson as needed.

The Treasurer

keeps accurate records, explains finances to the members, and at least once a year, presents a financial report to the membership.

- reads the records of expenditures for approval.

The Corresponding Secretary:

- writes all the letters for the group.
- sees that all notices of meetings reach all members.
- keeps files of all letters received.

The Parliamentarian:

- assists the chair in ruling on matters of policy relative to the Policy Council By-Laws.
- advises the chair of the presence of a quorum at the start of each regular meeting.
- Provides the chairperson with other assisstance when requested.
- Insures that proper parliamentary procedure in line with *Roberts' Rules of Order* is followed throughout every meeting.
- Participates in local, county, and state training programs.

Guide to Writing Better Minutes

1. Keep the minutes in a permanent book.

2. Leave enough space on sides and between lines for corrections.

3. Always include: the name of the group, whether it is a regular or a special meeting, the time, date, and place of the meeting, the name of the presiding officer, and the name of the secretary. If it is a small group, the names of those present.

4. Record all business briefly and without personal comment.

5. Record motions in full and include:
   A. The name of the maker of the motion.
   B. The motion itself.
   C. The action taken.

6. Do include all defeated motions.

7. Do not include everything that is said.

8. Write the minutes soon after the meeting.

9. Read minutes from the permanent copy; read slowly and clearly enough for people to listen.

Need for National Action for Policy

The Carnegie Council believes this country needs a national policy to empower parents with more resources and influence with which to raise their children. The following six themes are starting points or principles for discussion of a national policy issue:

1. Family Strengths and Supports. The family is the oldest, most fundamental human institution.

2. Diversity of Families. American families are pluralistic in nature.

3. The Changing Realities of Family Life. American society is dynamic and constantly changing.

4. The Impact of Public and Private Institutional Policies on Families.

5. The Impact of Discrimination. This affects individual family members as well as the family unit as a whole.

6. Families with Special Needs. Single-parents, the elderly, and the handicapped, have special needs and unique strengths.

Institutions have changed remarkably and become concerned with the needs and the problems of the poor and of the minorities. These concerns have been manifested by revising curricula, schedules, approaches, and services.

One cannot deny that in a short time, with a relatively small investment, Project Head Start has been a model and closely associated on a national basis with fundamental changes in educational and health institutions, two of the most crucial institutional groups in the country.

It is also clear that federal guidelines and federal money do not lead to monolithic, stereotyped programs, but do, in fact, encourage a variety of efforts on the local level. However, those in the field must face the problem of synthesizing and analyzing these efforts in order to make systematic recommendations to schools concerning the kinds of involvement that are the most effective (Nebgen, 1979).

Overall evidence of beneficial parent involvement is scanty, but one cannot conclude from this that such effect do not exist. In fact, a direct link has been found between parent involvement in the school and increased parent self-esteem and feelings of control.

Evaluation not only enables, but forces, the examination of the quality and value of the programs. Concern must be not only with how to do things more effectively, but also with why things are done and what happens as a result.

Information is the key to welding the home and school into a working unit. Making information available to the individual without question is the first step toward more open relationships. Teachers, school officials, parents, and children all have obligations and responsibilities. The more open and free the channels of communication, the more each participant will recognize and fulfill his responsibilities.

Present public policies affecting families are not always based on a realistic understanding of American families. Since most families are stressed at times, they will probably need social supports at some point in their life cycles. Furthermore, the ingrained concept of the ideal family being an isolated nucleus may discourage, if not actually prevent, some families from coping with stress in positive and unique ways (Boss, 1979).

Family Policy Models

Sweden, Israel, and France have strong national commitments to integrate women into the total society, to enrich early childhood development, and to strengthen the family, In addition, each of the nations has programs for young children and a comprehensive policy which supports the family thereby providing stability and security (Jordan, 1977).

A relatively sudden interest in family policy on the part of academicians and political leaders may offer new opportunities to enact social legislation. However, violations of civil liberties may threaten individuals and nonconventional families in the process. The risks of adopting a national policy for the family outweighs the possible gains and the risks are identified as those dealing with the role of the absent parent, deficiency in intact families, and degrees of need.

In the belief that there can be advantages to analyzing social policy in terms of its impact on families, Kamerman and Kahn (1970) present a case study in which they compare family policy in five European countries and the United States. The major question is how citizens can raise and care for children at the same time as they are productive members of the work force?

Adult Education Principles:
Andragogy vs. Pedagogy

Andragogy is defined as the art and science of helping adults learn, in contrast to pedagogy which is defined as the art and science of teaching children. An increasing andragogy is simply another model of assumptions about learners to be used beside the pedagogical model of assumptions, thereby providing two alternative models for testing assumptions. Furthermore, the models are probably most useful when seen not as dichotomous but rather as two ends of a spectrum, with a realistic assumption in a given situation falling somewhere between. For example, take the assumption of dependency versus self directedness. A six-year-old child may be highly self-directing in learning the rules of a game but quite dependent in learning to use a calculator. On the other hand, a forty-year-old adult may be very dependent in learning to program a computer but completely self-directing in learning to repair a piece of furniture. Whenever a pedagogical assumption is the realistic one, then pedagogical strategies are appropriate, regardless of the age of the learner, and vice versa. But there is one caveat: an ideological pedagogue— one who has a deep loyalty and commitment to the pedagogical model— may be tempted to underrate the extent to which an andragogical assumption may be realistic and may, for example, want to keep a learner dependent long after the learner is able to be self-directing.

Andragogy is premised on at least four crucial assumptions that are different from those on whch traditional pedagogy is premised. These assumptions are that, as an individual matures the self-concept moves from one of being a dependent personality toward being a self-directed individual; there accumulates a growing reservoir of experience that becomes an increasingly rich resource for learning; the readiness to learn becomes oriented increasingly to the developemental task of social roles; and time perspective changes from one of postponed application of knowledge to immediacy of application and, accordingly, the orientation toward learning shifts from one of subject-centeredness to one of performance-centeredness (Knowles, 1980).

A Comparison of the Assumptions
of Pedagogy and Andragogy

REGARDING:	PEDAGOGY	ANDRAGOGY
Concept of the learner	The role of the learner is, by definition, a dependent one. The teacher is expected by society to take full responsibility for determining what is to be learned, when it is to be learned, how it is to be learned, and if it has been learned.	It is a normal aspect of the process of maturation for a person to move from dependency toward increasing self-directedness, but at different rates for different people and in different dimensions of life. Teachers have a responsibility to encourage and nurture this movement. Adults have a deep psychological need to be generally self-directing, although they may be dependent in particular temporary situations.
Role of learners' experience	The experience learners bring to a learning situation is of little worth, It may be used as a starting point, but the experience from which learners will gain the most is that of the teacher, the textbook writer, the audio-visual aid producer, and other experts. Accordingly, the primary techniques in education are transmittal techniques — lecture, assigned reading, AV presentations.	As people grow and develop they accumulate an increasing reservoir of experience that becomes an increasingly rich resource for learning — for themselves and for others. Furthermore, people attach more meaning to learnings they gain from experience than those they acquire passively, Accordingly, the primary techniques in education are experiential techniques — laboratory experiments, discussion, problem-solving cases, simulation exercises, field experience, and the like.
Readiness to learn	People are ready to learn whatever society (especially the school) says they ought to learn, provided the pressures on them (like fear of failure) are great enough. Most people of the same age are ready to learn the same things. Therefore, learning should be organized into a fairly standardized curriculum, with a uniform step-by-step progression for all learners.	People become ready to learn something when they experience a need to learn it in order to cope more satisfyingly with real-life tasks or problems. The educator has a responsibility to create conditions and provide tools and procedures for helping learners discover their "need to know." And learning programs should be organized around life-application categories and sequenced according to the learners' readiness to learn.
Orientation to learning	Learners see education as a process of acquiring subject-matter content, most of which they understand will be useful only at a later time in life. Accordingly, the curriculum should be organized into subject-matter units (e.g., courses) which follow the logic of the subject (e.g., from ancient to modern history, from simple to complex mathematics or science). People are subject-centered in their orientation to learning.	Learners see education as a process of developing increased competence to achieve their full potential in life. They want to be able to apply whatever knowledge and skill they gain today to living more effectively tomorrow. Accordingly, learning experiences should be organized around competency-development categories. People are performance-centered in their orientation to learning.

Knowles (1980)

Needs of the Individual

The primary and immediate mission of every adult educator is to help individuals satisfy their needs and achieve their goals. Usually if an individual is asked what these needs and goals are, he or she will respond in terms of the acquisition of some specific competence, such as "being able to speak in public" or "knowing mathematics." Or the person might proceed to a higher level of abstraction and such objectives as "being able to make more money" or "being able to get along with people better." These, to be sure, are important incentives to learning but in this book they are treated as "interests" rather than "needs," a distinction that will be discussed fully in a later chapter. Interests are relevant to the adult educator's technology, but in relation to this mission we are talking about something different and more fundamental— indeed, something individuals are less conscious of than their interests— the more ultimate needs and goals of human fulfillment.

One such need can be stated negatively as the prevention of obsolescence. This need arises from the fact that most adults alive today were educated according to the doctrine that learning is primarily a function of youth and that the purpose of education is to supply individuals in their youth with all the knowledge and skills they will require to live adequately for the rest of their lives. But the rapidly accelerating pace of change in our society has invalidated this doctrine. Facts learned in youth have become insufficient and, in many instances, actually untrue; skills learned in youth have become outmoded by new technologies. Consequently, adult years become years of creeping obsolescence in work, play, understanding of oneself, and understanding the world.

The problem is that education is not yet perceived as a lifelong process, so people are still taught during their youth only what they should know then. They are not taught how to keep finding new information. One mission of the adult educator can be stated positively as helping individuals to develop the attitude that learning is a lifelong process and to acquire the skills of self-directed learning. In this sense, one of the tests of everything the adult educator does, whether it be to conduct a course in hatmaking, a workshop in human-relations, or a staff meeting, is the extent to which the participants leave a given experience with heightened curiosity and increased ability to carry on their own learning.

Another ultimate need of individuals is to achieve complete self-identity through the full development of their potentialities. Increasing evidence is appearing in the psychological literature that complete self-development is a universal human need, and that at least a feeling of movement in this direction is a condition of mental health.

A third ultimate need of individuals is to mature. Harry Overstreet equated maturity with "linkages with life." "A mature person is not one who has come to a certain level of achievement and stopped there. He is rather a maturing person whose linkages with life are constantly becoming stronger and richer because his attitudes are such as to encourage their growth. . . . A mature person, for example, is not one who knows a large number of facts. Rather, he is one whose mental habits are such that he grows in knowledge and the wise use of it."

The idea of maturity as a goal of education must be defined more specifically than this, however, if it is to serve as a guide to continuous learning. From social-psychological literature comes the idea that there are several dimensions of the maturing process, each with its own unique cycle of development. If the really critical dimensions of maturation could be identified, adult educators would have some reliable yardsticks against which to measure their accomplishment.

The concept of maturing can be made clearer by these explanations as summarized from Erikson's theories (1950):

1. From dependence toward autonomy. All human beings enter this world in a completely dependent condition; their every need must be fulfilled by someone else. One of the central quests of life is for increasing self-direction, although the opposite of dependence in our complicated world may not be independence so much as it may be self-directing interdependence.

2. From passivity toward activity. Throughout childhood individuals become increasingly active in exploring the world about them and tend to engage in an expanding number of activities. In adulthood the emphasis is likely to shift from quantitative activity to qualitative activity. The way children are taught to participate in school and in other educative experiences, whether as passive recipients of knowledge or as active inquirers after knowledge, will greatly affect the direction and speed of their growth.

3. From subjectivity toward objectivity. It is a universal characteristic of infancy that the world revolves around "me," takes on its meaning from "my" perception of it, and is subject to "my" commands. One of the most difficult adjustments people have to make in life is to move themselves from the center of the universe to discover where they really fit. The extent to which each experience in life helps them look at themselves realistically and maintain self-respect in the process is certainly one of the tests of its educational quality.

4. From ignorance toward enlightenment. It is in this area of maturing that schooling has traditionally placed its emphasis. People should be perceived as both specialists and generalists. As specialists, people need to master the knowledge and skills of their vocations. But as generalists they need to keep up to date on knowledge from all specialities that bear on the practical problems of life. This suggests a kind of "core curriculum" for adult education, which would consist of a distillation of the essential elements from every discipline.

5. From small abilities toward large abilities. Once one has learned to do something well, there is a tendency to take pride in that ability and to rest on the laurels it creates. Since each newly developed ability is learned in its simplest form, this tendency can result in individuals becoming locked into the lowest level of their potential performance.

6. From few responsibilities toward many responsibilities. Another curious tendency in human nature, especially among parents, teachers, and supervisors, is to underestimate the amount of responsibility a child, student, or subordinate can assume. Thus, the maturation process is frequently retarded by the parent retaining responsibility the child is prepared to take over, or the teacher making decisions the students are ready to make, or the supervisor carrying out functions the subordinates are ready to have delegated to them.

7. From narrow interests toward broad interests. The child's world starts with a field of interests bounded by the crib. One significant sign of a person's continuing maturation is the extension of this field in ever-widening circles for the rest of his life. Anything that causes an individual's field of interests to become fixed within a given circle or to recede to smaller circles is interfering with an important dimension of maturation. This dimension has special relevance to work done with older people. There is a widely held myth that it is natural for interests to diminish with age. Gerontologists who have made the opposite assumption, that older people are able to develop new interests and are healthier if they do, have had spectacular results.

8. From selfishness toward altruism. People are born into the world in a state of total self-centeredness, so one of the central tasks for the rest of their lives is to become increasingly able to care about others. Conditions that induce a spirit of rivalry rather than helpfulness, such as the competition for grades promoted by traditional schooling, interfere with maturation in this dimension. There are some psychiatrists who believe that altruism is the single best criterion of mental health.

9. From self-rejection to self-acceptance. While children's first impressions of themselves are probably that they are kings or queens they soon learn that much of their natural behavior (making noise, getting into things, not eating correctly, etc.) is "bad." Their attitudes then quickly change from self-adulation to self-rejection. Mature persons are those who accept themselves as persons of worth, which is a prerequisite to being able to accept others. The extent to which subsequent life experiences help the individual move from self-rejection toward self-acceptance will largely determine whether or not an individual will mature in this dimension.

10. From amorphous self-identity toward integrated self-identity. Erik Erikson has provided the deepest insights into this dimension of maturation, through the "eight ages of man" concept as follows:

    a. oral-sensory, in which the basic issue is trust vs. mistrust

    b. muscular-anal, in which the basic issue is autonomy vs. shame

    c. locomotion-genital, in which the basic issue is initiative vs. guilt

    d. latency, in which the basic issue is industry vs. inferiority

    e. puberty and adolescence, in which the basic issue is identity vs. role confusion

    f. young adulthood, in which the basic issue is intimacy vs. isolation

    g. adulthood, in which the basic issue is generativity vs. stagnation

    h. maturity, in which the basic issue is ego-integrity vs. despair

    Although no stage is completely fulfilled at any point in life, we continue to actualize each stage further throughout life. If development in a given stage is mostly frustrated, an individual is likely to remain fixed at that stage. The dimension of maturation from "I don't know who I am" toward "I know clearly who I am" is a delicate and crucial one.

11. From focus on particulars toward focus on principles. To a child's mind, each object is unique and each event is unconnected with any other. The discovery of principles enabling a person to group objects and connect events is the essence of the process of inquiry. One of the tragic aspects of traditional pedagogy is that it has so often imposed principles on inquiring minds and has therefore denied them the opportunity to mature in the ability to discover principles.

12. From superficial concerns toward deep concerns. The young child's world is an existential world; all that matters is the enjoyment of pleasure and the avoidance of pain at the moment. One dimension of maturation consists of gaining a perspective on what mattered more deeply in our past and is likely to matter more deeply in our future. Having accomplished this feat, we can gain perspective on what matters in the past and the future of others. Too often this process is retarded by society's imposition of its deep concerns on individuals before they have discovered their own.

13. From imitation toward originality. The child's first technique of learning and adpating is that of imitation. The adult world has long tended to accept this method of learning as not only natural but best, and has geared much of its educational system to produce conformity through imitation. The consequence has been the retardation of generations of human beings toward the more self-fulfilling end of this dimension, originality.

14. From the need for certainty toward tolerance for ambiguity. The basic insecurity of the world imposes a deep need for certainty. Only as experiences in life provide us with an increasing sense of security and self-confidence will we be able to move in the direction of a mature tolerance for ambiguity, which is a prerequisite for survival in a world of ambiguity.

15. From impulsiveness toward rationality. Traditionally, the naturally impulsive behaviors of children have been controlled through systems of reward and punishment— with emphasis on the latter. Too often the consequence of this policy is a reaction of irrationality, rebellion, withdrawal, and fantasy. True maturing toward rationality requires self-understanding and control of one's impulses.

Perhaps there are other dimensions of the maturing process that ought to be added or that ought to replace some of these dimensions; certainly, until further research is done on this important aspect of human development, we shall have to regard any such formulation as highly tentative. In the meantime, the general notion that one of the missions of the adult educator is to assist individuals to continue maturing throughout life provides some useful guidelines for the development of a sequential, continuous, and integrated program of lifelong learning (Erikson, 1950).

Application Activities

1. Through a group or class, practice the various procedures in conducting a meeting.
2. Attend a parent group (for example, Parents Without Partners, Parent Cooperative or PTA) meeting. Write minutes from the meeting and develop a set of conclusions relative to need and process.
3. Visit a Project Head Start program and interview the Parent Co-ordinator. Discuss all aspects of Project Head Start parent involvement and prepare a summary report. Include recommendations.
4. Participate in a local fund-raising campaign. Discuss the purpose of the campaign, the method in which the campaign was conducted, and the impact of campaign funds upon local families.
5. Visit a social service agency. Determine whether the climate of the agency is achievement, affiliation, or power-oriented. Prepare your conclusions and assumptions in a written report for class analysis.
6. Design a parents' bulletin board for use in an elementary school. Information for such a board might include lists of reliable baby sitters, community events, and clothing exchanges, as well as child care pamphlets and article reprints.
7. Create a parent newsletter. You might include such items as the upcoming school menu, information about parent meetings, and activities for parents and children.
8. Draft a model "family policy" statement indentifying issues and solutions.
9. Teach a group of parents how to conduct a meeting using *Robert's Rules of Order*. Prepare handouts and document the process and outcomes.
10. Interview a school board member or a school superintendent about his perceptions of or opinion about parent involvement.
11. Conduct a survey of three elementary schools to ascertain the types and amounts of parent participation. Document.
12. Work as a volunteer at a local day care center, school, or hospital. Report on your experiences.
13. Design a questionnaire and interview at least five working mothers about their attitudes toward the local day care situation.
14. Write your state representative to obtain his or her views on parent involvement in education as well as information about pending legislation regarding parents as educators.
15. Organize a training session for a group of parents. Describe:

a. the chosen topic and why you chose it
b. the training plan selected
c. the response to the training session
d. the changes necessary to make a more successful session
16. Attend at least three different parent group meetings. Compare and contrast the leaders at each meeting.

Bibliography

Bladley, M. 1981. Special child advocates: A volunteer court program. *Children Today*, 10: 2 – 6.

Boss, P. 1979. Theoretical influences on family policy. *Journal of Home Economics*, 71: 17 – 21.

Della, Dora, D. 1978. Changing styles of leadership. *The Education Leadership*, 35: 6 – 7.

Coughlin, P., (exec. ed.). 1977. *Nuggets*. From the 1977 National Head Start Workshop. Project Head Start. P.O. Box 1182, Washington, D.C. 20013.

Erikson, E.H. 1950. *Childhood and Society*. New York: W.W. Norton.

Granowsky, A., et. al. 1977. How to put parents in your classroom team. *Instructor*, 87: 54 – 62.

Guttman, J.A. 1978. "Getting parents involved in preschool." *Education Digest*. 44: 15 – 17.

Hoppe, P. 1979. How to organize self-help groups in the schools. *The Exceptional Parent*, 9: E22 – 23.

Jordon, R. 1977. A Commitment to children. A Report of the Coalition of Labor Union Women Child Care Seminar. Sponsored by the German Marshall Fund of the United States, 1977.

Kamerman, S.B., and Kahn, A.J. Comparative analysis in family policy: A case study. *Social Work*, 24: 506 – 12.

Kappelman, M., and Ackerman, P. 1977. Between parent and school. *The Exceptional Parent*. 7: 15 – 16.

Knowles, M.S. 1980. *The Modern Practice of Adult Education*. Association Press. Follett Publishing Co., Chicago.

Marburger, C.L. 1980. Parents/citizens: The fourth force in education. *NASSP Bulletin*, 64: 8 – 13.

Nebgen, M.K. 1979. Parent involvement in Title I programs. *The Educational Forum.* 43: 165 – 73.

Pealman, E., and Williams, J. 1980. Summary of the head and home start parent questionnaire results from 1977 – 1980. Mt. Vernon, Ohio Head Start. November, 1 – 12.

Romanofsky, P., (ed.). 1978. *Social service agency.* Vol. #1, Greenwood Press.

Scott-Blair, R.M. 1978. The changing PTA: No more tea and cookies and maybe no more T. *Learning*, 6: 68 – 70.

Sparling, V. 1980. PTA involvement in the '80s: New concepts, new directions. *NASSP Bulletin.* Vol: 64: 23 – 29.

Sponberg, H. 1948. *Parliamentary procedure.* Cooperative Extension Service. Michigan State University, East Lansing, Michigan.

Sponberg, H. 1980. *Parent Handbook* (4th edition). Out Wayne Co. Head Start. Way County Intermediate School District, Wayne, Michigan. Schuster, New York.

7. *Parents of Special Children*

Generalization

Incidence of disabilities in schools constitutes a significant population, often estimated at ten percent. These special situations, problems or handicaps likely impair the individual's ability to function. Parent counseling, which is part of the overall thrust and goals of parent education, can be effective in the amelioration of many of these problems (Loveless, 1981).

New opportunities have emerged because of behind-the-scenes lobbying for exceptional children. These groups have steadfastly worked to guarantee more opportunities for exceptional children and their parents. Courts have granted these children and their parents relief by removing the restrictions which inadvertently compounded the handicapping conditions.

The past systems perpetuated handicappedness on the part of children and fear on the part of their parents. Now, the growing realization is that change is indeed here, and that it is presenting to exceptional children and their families more opportunities than even the most optimistic of advocates had thought possible (Fanning, 1977).

Objectives

1. To discuss federal legislation PL-142, which provides legal action in support of handicapped children as interpreted in PL 94-142

2. To professionally explain the rationale and systems for working with parents of handicapped children

3. To present information with which parents can be educated to better understand respective "special need" and "gifted" children

4. To explain and discuss various innovative counseling efforts for parents of special and gifted children

5. To explore "parent feelings" relative to special needs and gifted children as a way of increasing the professional student's awareness for working with parents

Parent Involvement with Special Children

Parent involvement is beneficial to all children and particularly to those who are exceptional. According to Peters and Stephenson (1979), the primary need of exceptional children is to have their parents involved, thereby increasing their awareness in several important areas. First, parents need to understand the sensitive and complex interaction between learning, facing problems, and a child' self esteem. Second is the need for parents to learn modes of child management that emphasize positive patterns of interaction, sensitive listening, and social reinforcement. Third, parents can reinforce the cognitive and social skills introduced in the classroom and clinic by providing practice in the home and other parts of the natural environment.

Professionals need to be very cautious about judging or condemning parents and should not forget that it is hard for parents to seek advice about education. Instinctive love does not help parents overcome difficulties in educating their children. Parents are usually laymen in the field of education, and their experience in dealing with the exceptional child is normally limited to their own child. Since education is becoming more complicated in these days of social disruption, professional parent educators and other "special" educators must be sensitive to parents' feelings while designing appropriate training programs to better help them understand their own children.

Attitudes of Parents

The parents' attitudes toward the education of children with special problems can be the deciding factor in whether the program is a success. It should compliment the teacher's role and even make the teacher's role easier (Love, 1970).

How parents respond to the crisis of the birth of a special child is determined by many factors. How they were parented themselves and their abilities and experiences in coping with stress of any type will influence their response to their special child. The quality and value of the educational support system (Goldson, 1979) can be an extremely important influence.

PL 94-142

The Education for All Handicapped Children Act (PL 94-142) still holds promise for children in need, for their parents, and for caring teachers. The act is intended to involve parents in the education of their children because parents have the ultimate responsibility for their children.

Parents Rights

Public Law PL 94-142, enacted November 1975, guarantees a free public education to any handicapped child. Through this law, parents are protected by having:

1. the right to deny permission for any proposed evaluation activities — teacher needs written consent of parents

2. the right to review and inspect all records upon which educational decisions are made, to obtain a copy of such records at actual cost of copying, and to request amendments to be made to the data

3. the right to obtain an independent evaluation of the child at their own expense and introduce such information into the child's records

4. the right to present to the superintendent of the school district complaints with respect to the evaluation or educational placement of the child or the provision of special education

5. the right to due process hearing conducted by an impartial hearing officer including:
   - advice by counsel
   - evidence and use of witnesses
   - record of hearings
   - findings of fact and decisions

6. the right to be fully informed in written and oral form of all proposed evaluations, placements, and periodic review activities, and decisions

7. the right to obtain a description of the kinds and numbers of facilities, program options, services, and personnel provided

8. the right to have a conference with any person participating in education decisions during the evaluation, placement, and/or periodic review process.

Child's Rights

1. All the rights of the parent shall pass to the child upon reaching the age of the majority except in cases where the child is legally determined under state statute to be incompetent.

Due Process

1. Parents shall be notified of the intent to identify and formally evaluate any child suspected of needing special education.

2. Within fifteen days after the receipt of the placement team conference report, the superintendent shall notify the parent by certified mail that a change in the educational status of the child is proposed or denied.

3. Personally identifiable data procedural safeguards require that parents receive prior notice of the confidentiality of data and be given access to personally identifiable or other pertinent data concerning the evaluation and placement of child.

4. Periodic review suggests that no later than twelve months, the school district shall conduct a review of the child's individual educational program to evaluate it. Parents must be notified fifteen days prior to this. (Standards for Special Education, Ohio Department of Education, Columbus, Ohio).

Mainstreaming

Today, as compared with the past, official policy reflects a complete about-face. Rather than isolate retarded persons, every effort is being made to keep them in the mainstream of normal living and to allow them, as far as possible, to grow up with their families. The public also now regards special people with far more tolerance and, although prejudice still exists, there is an increasing awareness that they have the same need for love and acceptance as all persons.

"Mainstreaming" is the current term for the least restrictive placement concept but it has been widely misinterpreted. The act assures that to the maximum extent appropriate, handicapped children will be educated with children who are not handicapped. However, "to the extent appropriate" is often ignored. Mainstream placements should not be made without using common sense to identify and address the specific needs of the individual child and to re-evaluate remedial developmental programs the child has had in the past and which may still be needed.

For example, a thirteen-year-old learning disabled child who was mainstreamed in a junior high school was given a regular schedule of reading and written reports. He attempted this schedule despite an evaluation report of dyslexia and very poor fine motor skills. As a result, the child developed severe colitis. Physical and emotional illnesses may be negative side effects of indiscriminate placements. Some parents report increased bed-wetting, colitis, and diarrhea as children struggle to cope with their placements in sometimes hostile school settings (Hanley, 1979).

There are progressive attempts by dedicated educators to place handicapped children in programs in self-contained classes and in regular classrooms. It is too early to assess the outcomes of these efforts but something positive is happening. The success is mostly at the elementary school level where teachers are more child-oriented and not so restricted by subject curriculum, which is rarely modified to suit the needs of mainstreamed children.

Hanley (1979) continues to explain that another important variable is the poor quality of individualized educational programs (IEPs). Developing IEPs is a time-consuming and costly process. They might have been the redeeming factor in the act's implementation except that schools caught in a compliance crunch failed to ensure that the IEPs were qualified plans. Parents often rubber-stamp efforts written by teachers who had never seen their children, by speech therapists for education programs, and by a host of other school personnel. If the IEP was to have been a prescription for learning, specifying the areas to be remediated as well as the methodology, it should have been written by those who had evaluated and tested the child and who had consulted with the parents for further input. In some school systems teachers and parents now refer to IEP compliance documents as a "paper dragon."

Guidelines for Action

Parents will not be helped a great deal by simply providing them with paper guidelines for action. Rather, genuine help through special support parent education programs must provide them with the opportunity for bringing to light and exploring all the unhappy feelings they have not been able to face and to identify actions through which these feelings can be resolved.

Heisler (1972) reports that although reality factors are obviously present and important in attempting to understand parental feelings toward the child, these factors alone are quite insufficient to account for the gamut of perceptions and feelings which parents show. Many unconscous factors also seem to affect their attitudes and behaviors. It would therefore be erroneous to base planning for the needs of the handicapped child and his family upon reality factors alone. This view is that the best way to facilitate family adjustment to the special handicap of a child is through a combination of education and psychotherapy. The advantage of a therapy group is that it enables the parents to help each other with problems specific to the handicap and not shared by the general population. This sharing breaks through the sense of isolation that surrounds those who have children with special problems. The kind of inner adjustment a person makes to one experience of frustration will affect his ability to meet the next frustration.

One of the most important things parents can give the handicapped child is recognition and respect for the individual that he is. Parents harm a child by blocking his potential, two of the most common ways being pushing and overprotecting. Both make it more difficult for the child to discover and develop his own resources. Overprotection holds the child back by interfering with his initiative and taking away his courage. Pushing the child interferes with his initiative by taking away his opportunity for motivation at his respective level of readiness.

Education alone will not have all the answers. The handicapped child must also be given opportunities to socialize and identify with nonhandicapped peers and other individuals outside of his home. Friendships cannot develop if there is no contact (Heisler, 1972).

The knowledge base of parents must also be increased. It can be quite useful for parents occasionally to attend courses on matters of education to inform themselves about the developmental phases of their children. Parents of disabled children should have group leaders with professional psychotherapy or group counseling skills, and these group leaders should have a full body of knowledge about learning disabilities. The educator-counselor must also identify with the parents' emotions and experiences while maintaining a non-judgmental attitude. Negative or anxiety-laden feelings toward children with handicaps are healthy reactions to stress, and each group session should provide periods for silence to let parents recollect past experiences and work on problem-solving. A combination of the above will enable parents of the learning disabled child to gain insights, to strengthen their child's opportunities for learning, and to become familiar with personal and professional attitudes.

Disability and Learning

The "special" situations described in the following pages are the most common and primarily those that impede the education process but not totally inclusive of all forms of disability. These brief descriptions should serve to increase the awareness of parent educators and to provide parents with basic knowledge for educating further research and/or communicating with special education teachers and counselors.

Disabilities of Special Children

Special children who are identified as having mental-emotional problems may have characteristics of even yet a wider range of particular disabilities. While Greene (1983) identifies these as "learning problems," Loveless (1981) categorizes disabilities in a broader sense. The respective breakdowns are:

Greene	Loveless
1. Neurological Disorders	1. Physical— Motor
2. Sensory Impairment	A. Hearing
3. Language Disorders	B. Language
4. Mental Retardation	C. Vision
5. Cultural Deprivation	D. Orthopedic
6. Language Deficiency	2. Behavioral
7. Emotional Problems	A. Overactive
	B. Withdrawn
	3. Developmental Delay
	4. Learning Disabilities
	5. Economic
	6. Child Abuse and Neglect

Perceptual decoding skills of auditory processing and language encoding skills are those manifested in neurological disorders. These conditions also relate to causes of language disability. According to Greene (1983), when a child has a sensory condition, receptors (sight or hearing) are defective. "Unlike the language disorder in which the brain has difficulty associating thoughts with the verbal symbols that are expressing these thoughts, speech disorders involve either a physiological deficit which interferes with the production of sound or an inability to use the muscles or organs that produce sound efficiency" (p. 56).

Mental Retardation

Mental retardation has many causes both before and after birth. Some of these include heredity, nutrition, living conditions, emotions, physical factors, interpersonal relationships, and environment. There are four different classifications of retarded individuals in accordance with the degrees of retardation. The mildly retarded person or EMR (educably mentally retarded) develops slower than the average child, but he can be educated, employed, and is capable of living an independent life. He has an intelligence quotient (IQ) of 55 to 70. The moderately retarded person or TMR (trainably mentally retarded) person is trainable but slow in development. He will probably always need to live and work in a sheltered environment. He will have an IQ of 25 to 55. The severely retarded person or PMR (profoundly mentally retarded) will have trouble in speech, language, and motor development. A profoundly retarded individual needs constant care and supervision. He has gross impairment of physical and sensory development and coordination. He is very often physically handicapped and has an IQ of less that 20 (HEW, 1975, and Greene, 1983).

Cultural disabilities are those that, because of a lack of understanding of the English language, leaves the child socially dysfunctional.

Emotional problems may not always be distinctly different from a learning problem but may seriously complicate the learning process. Often poor self-concept and behavior problems are associated with emotional problems.

In comparison to their relationship to a normal child, parents are often observed to demonstrate less affection toward the child with emotional problems, to give him less approval, and to be generally more rejecting of him as an individual and a member of the family (Greene, 1983).

Counseling parents of an emotionally disturbed child differs from working with parents of other exceptional children. Because the parents have contributed to the development of the disorder, their influence must be understood and neutralized if the child's disturbance is to be relieved and its recurrence prevented. Moreover, the parent must change if the situation or malady is to be corrected.

An emotionally disturbed child is not likely to complain openly about his worries. Instead, he may become depressed, lose interest in activities, seek new friends, and become unusually quiet. Others may become overanxious, cry a lot, sleep badly, and cling to their parents. Unruly behavior, too, may be a sign of disturbance as the child tries to draw attention to his problems. Children with phobias transfer their real fears to situations or objects with symbolic value while other children suffer from hysterical illnesses, converting an emotional problem into a physical problem. Parents can sometimes help a child through a difficult period, but if the difficulties are prolonged or severe, professional help may be needed.

Peters and Stephenson (1979) state "parents are encouraged to openly explore ways to alter the child's environment or their relationship with one another or to their child in order to foster feelings of self esteem in their child."

Developmental Delay

Children who are not considered retarded but who exhibit various learning problems are often described as having maturational lag or being developmentally delayed.

In learning to read, the term "maturational lag" is often concerned with perceptual immaturity, often with the additional factor of emotional stress. Immaturity may also be evident in behavioral responses to problems. Outbursts of frustration or shortness of attention may be part of the total picture. Often the child who is having trouble mastering written language is extremely verbal and has no trouble at all with oral expression. It is particularly difficult for parents to understand this peculiar difference in regard to skills that are obviously related.

Parental Reactions

Interventions on behalf of the child require careful study of the family as a whole. If the disturbed child serves to maintain family equilibrium, removing him from the home will result in family disequilibrium. Reciprocal and mutual impact of the child on his family and of the family on the child must be studied if the disorders of these children are to be fully understood. The effect the child has on parents in their parental role behavior is determined in large measure by the parent's own individual psychodynamics and their relations as marital partners.

Goldson (1979) states, "the birth of a sick infant, however he be premature, deformed or seriously ill, presents an even greater crisis in that it challenges all the goals and expectations that the parents have had prior to conception and during the pregnancy." Briston (1984) believes that parents must grieve and that this process may take many months or even longer before they can establish an attachment to the sick infant. Along with this will be much guilt.

Understandably, parents must call on a variety of family and community resources. Plus, their own abilities to cope and their attitudes toward the baby, each other, and the marriage will greatly influence the establishment of a normal parent-child relationship.

The developmental stages that parents go through in adapting to the birth of a sick infant are: stage one, preparing for the fact that the child may die; stage two, accepting the situation; stage three, the resuming their interactive relationship with the baby; and stage four, realizing the special needs of the sick infant (Kaplan and Mason 1960).

The Drotar et al. (1975) theory of parental reaction suggests that at first parents are in a state of shock followed by denial. Next they become angry and then they begin to adapt. This is normally followed by reorganization.

Goldson (1979) suggests that clinicians can be helpful and that "we should observe more than the superficial behaviors of parents. . . be sensitive and learn how to support parents through this crisis and to remain a continual source of support."

The Gifted Child

The approach to parents of a gifted child is essentially no different from the approach to parents of children with other exceptional states. Counseling help the parents to a clear and accurate perception of reality so that their relationship to the child can be free of distorted perceptions and disrupting conflicts. In order to do his work, the counselor or parent educator must be fully acquainted with the local resources. Through interviews and testing, he must explore the needs of the specific family so that his consultation can indeed be oriented to reality. Finally, the counselor must have explored his own attitudes toward gifted children. Professionals, no less so than the general public, are likely to react to a gifted child with hostile envy, and the counselor must recognize and manage his own feelings before he can help his clients.

Gallagher (1975) states, "the gifted are almost invariably more popular and more socially accepted than children at other levels of intellectual ability." Traits labeled characteristics of eminence could be used to describe these persons: trustworthy, conscientious, influential, self-confident, self-perceptive, quick of apprehension, profound of apprehension, creative, and forceful. In addition, Gallagher (1975) found that the gifted possessed extraordinary leadership, common sense, keen observation, and perseverance or "quiet determination." Gallagher (1975) continues to explain that contemporary researchers and educators have cited the following additional traits common to gifted and talented individuals: curiosity, extensive vocabulary, good reading ability, persistence, good health and coordination, concern about world issues and problems, high goals and high expectations of self and others, mature sense of humor, ability to make unusual but valid associations and relationships, and interest in many areas.

Traits of gifted individuals fall into six areas: general intellectual ability, specific academic aptitude, creative or productive thinking, leadership ability, visual and performing arts, and psychomotor ability. A gifted individual is one who possesses exceptional abilities in any of these areas, either singly or in combination. In this way, gifted and talented individuals are grouped under one umbrella, although some educators still distinguish between the two categories.

Being the parent of a gifted child can be awesome, ego threatening, challenging, a chance to "shine" vicariously, a blessing, or a curse. The parent who sees giftedness as a challenge, one that is not to be exploited but is to provide opportunities for growth, is the parent most likely to succeed in helping the gifted child become a mentally healthy adult. To meet this challenge, relevant skills are needed. Supplying an optimum opportunity for the healthy development of a child's gifts requires skills in parenting, skills that can be learned if not already present.

Counseling Approaches

According to Hackney (1981) one of the function of educators is to counsel. He states "by developing the roles of communicator, mediator, and educator to the interface of family systems and the school as a system, the counselor's role becomes one of positive intervention and constructive involvement. The natural consequence is that both systems stand to benefit" (p. 54).

Colangelo and Dettman (1980) outline one counseling model for parents of gifted children. It can generally be applied to all special children and is as follows:

Parent-Centered Approach

Assumptions
- Parents are responsible for intellectual and affective development of child.

- Home environment is most important to development of gifted.

- Parents should seek outside experts or provide for enrichment activities if they feel child needs them.

Role of Counselor
- Provide information and advice as to what parents can do.

- Encourage parents to actively seek suitable experiences for child.

Role of Parent
- Be active in providing for their child.

- Role is as active as financial sources and parent interest will allow.

School-Centered Approach

Assumptions
- School is responsible for intellectual and affective education of child.

- School environment is most important.

- School should establish appropriate programs.

Role of Counselor
- Provide for needs of gifted.

- Help parents see that needs of gifted can be best met through experts and school programs.

Role of Parents
- Be passive participants, not seen as a teacher for their children.

- Role of parents is essentially confined to parent/school organizations.

Partnership Approach

Assumptions
- Counselors have expertise that can be beneficial to parents of gifted.

- Parents of gifted have knowledge and expertise that the counselor and school need to understand child.

- Parents are partners with educators in meeting educational and affective needs of gifted.

- Parents, with help of counselor, can be actively involved in the learning process of their child.

Role of Counselor and Parent
- Parents and counselors work as a team.

- Counselor provides information to parents and elicits information about child.

- Parents and counselor make joint decisions on best way to meet educational needs of gifted.

Bricklin's Counseling Model

A model psychoeducational counseling approach has been provided by Bricklin (1970). Basically she suggests that during counseling sessions, specific information be provided by the counselor. Parents ask questions about the nature, etiology, and prognosis of the learning disabilities. The sessions also constitute a forum where parents can express their feelings toward the children and the school. A coordinated approach between home and school is thereby established. Parents are helped to understand the feelings that generate various behaviors in their children and parents are taught to become accurate listeners and observers of their children so as to know what their behaviors are really saying. More important, however, parents are encouraged to decide what they want their children to learn before they respond to the behaviors.

If parents are not ready for group counseling, individual counseling is advocated until such time as they are ready. Grouping parents who have children of similar ages and who have similar problems is recommended. Initially, leader participation is great. As sessions progress to areas involving feelings, leader participation diminishes.

Counseling Conditions

Warmth denotes neither approval nor disapproval of any particular action, but rather a valuing of or caring for the individual as a person. This is communicated for the most part through nonverbal behavior[4]. A touch, a smile, a concerned look, or a particular tone of voice can show a caring attitude. The very fact that an individual listens to another attentively with the whole presence demonstrates this value system.

Empathy is feeling with another or imaginative transposing of oneself into the thinking, feeling, and acting of another. The teacher can do this primarily by responding to parents in a way that lets them know that the teacher heard and understood what they were trying to communicate— both content and behavior reflect the teacher's sincere effort to understand the individual parent.

Respect is based on a belief that parents have the capability to solve their own problems. Respect is communicated by not denying the individual parent a particular perception of the child or of a problem. The fact that the parent's perspective may differ from the teacher's does not mean it is wrong, nor does it mean that the two cannot reach a mutual understanding. But judging or denying the parent's perception will most certainly have damaging effects. Respect also means not doing for parents what they can do for themselves; it means supporting them in a collaborative way in their effort.

Correctness is the ability to be specific in communicating. The teacher can be concrete by reinforcing parents' attempts to be specific in discussing their problems that relate to the conference goals. In this way the teacher demonstrates a willingness to help parents with their concerns regardless of positive or negative connotations. For the teacher, this involve placing understanding above self-defense; seeking meaning for both parties to replace frustration, anger, or pessism; and cutting through to the sources of these feelings.

Honesty is the teacher's ability to be real, to be congruent— not performing a role or dutifully carrying our a directive, but being genuinely involved with the parents. There must be a harmony between feelings, and verbal and nonverbal behavior. The teacher can communicate this quite simply be meaning that what he/she says and saying what he/she means, still mindful of the best interests of all parties.

Closely related is *self-disclosure*, which is the ability to convey relevant personal experiences that may help parents realize they are not alone with their problems, that others have had similar experiences and have found solutions.

Immediacy is pointing out what is taking place between parent and teacher in the present relationship. It is threatening because of its present focus on the parties involved in the conference. Parents may exhibit a range of feelings and attitudes directed not toward the problem or conference topic but toward the teacher. This happens because the parent may be afraid to failing in some task with the child, and thus he or she gives way to frustration and anger. The teacher can communicate immediacy by understanding and discussing these feelings.

Confrontation is pointing out discrepancies between enacted and verbal behaviors, self- and ideal concepts, insight and action, potential and present behaviors. It can be threatening, but if used correctly confrontation can lead to growth, change, and problem solving. Positive aspects should be stressed in conferences— that is, one's potential (Rotter and Robinson, 1982).

Principles of Interviewing

There are principles which can be learned and knowledge which can be communicated, but only the practical application of principles and knowledge can develop a person who will eventually be able to help others through the use of the interview. An interview is a verbal exchange between two or more persons; it is not a conversation. An interview, in the context here under discussion, is a directed communication between a person in helping role and a person or persons who are seeking his help.

In a helping relationship which uses interview as the principal tool, the counselor hopes to render the parent's ego capable of an undistorted perception of reality so that he can make reality-oriented decisions. The interview with parents of exceptional children may have a variety of purposes, depending on the stage of the contract.

According to Ross (1964), the individual responsible for working with parents must have a basic understanding of human development principle; he must also be able to appreciate and accept behaviors that are ambivalent and values that are different from his own. Further, the interactions between the professional and the parent must emerge from the parents' experience during the course of the interview. The counselor must allow the parent to set the opening topic, he must place questions carefully and be able to free the parents' ego so that the result is a clear and undistorted perception of reality as it affects their child.

Parental Potential

Parents of all children, and particularly parents of children who are special, must realize that their ability to observe, perceive, and interpret situations and to convert these abilities into solutions for their child is an extremely important strength.

Many disabilities are multiple and range from moderate to severe (Greene, 1983). They affect all aspect of family — physical, emotional, home management, use of space and use of all other resources. In order to cope with these manifestations, parents must be ingenious, assertive, tolerant, energetic and persistent.

Parent groups appear to offer great help to their members in overcoming the feelings of isolation and frustration. Those who work with handicapped children and their families know that most childhood handicaps present a many-faceted problem that requires a multidisciplinary approach to the search for solutions. It is also important that the encouragement that comes from knowing that one's problem is not unique.

Five parental coping strategies are discussed by Turnbull et al. (1984), three external and two internal. Those classified as external are social support; the ability to acquire and used assistance from extended family, friends and neighbors; spiritual support, the ability to acquire and use spiritual interpretation, advice from religious leaders, and participation in religious activities; and formal support, the ability to acquire and use community resources and professional assistance.

Internal strategies are passive appraisal, avoidance of problems based on the belief that they will resolve themselves over time; and reframing, the ability to identify conditions that can alter and initiate problem-solving and to identify conditions beyond one's control and make attitude adjustments for constructive living.

Brinton (1984) gives some very practical suggestions in that the parent's story needs to be told. This is effective in working through the sense of loss a family feels after the birth of a handicapped child. Even more practical is the suggestion that other children should be included in the grieving and that friends and counselors and time for self are important.

The principles of psychological health and adjustment do not vary according to the specific problem. The same principles of human functioning that mobilize any of life's challenges are mobilized by the problem of the handicapped and this concept can be equally applied to the child's and parent's adjustments.

The child's handicap imposes certain limitations which vary according to the nature and severity of the impairment. Thus, in addition to meeting the everyday challenges to psychological adjustment, the physically handicapped child must learn to manage his special deprivation and frustration and must maximize the potential for living within the framework of the disability. Success in this struggle will be determined by those factors which influence the personality and his level of psychological self-actualization. Psychologists have contributed to a widespread recognition that the family is the primary agent in forming personality patterns. In ways about which they are most often unconscious, parents create their child's formative experiences, and the significant interchanges are more often psychological rather than directly observable. The kind of person the parent is also constitutes a powerful influence. Only by recognizing the power of unconscious activities and taking them into account can one extend one's sphere of conscious awareness and control.

Who then has the responsibility to help? There is, first of all, no one professional who can claim the exclusive right to counseling parents of exceptional children. Every professional who comes into contact with parents has the responsibility to help and to remember that he is dealing with a whole child and his family. This does not mean that every professional should therefore enter into a counseling relationship; it means that everyone must operate on the basis of the one overriding principle of all healthy interpersonal relations: the concept of honesty (Ross, 1964).

Working With Families

Professionals who work with parents should be prepared to meet their needs for belonging, self-esteem, and information. Without question, educators and other professionals will have to continue their advocacy roles to assist parents of both gifted and handicapped children in pursuing prescribed actions. Parents are typically unwilling to undertake these assignments without the help of a committed responsible professional.

Teachers should continually seek to mobilize the energy of parents toward productive ends. Parent educators should help parents find satisfaction in learning what can be done for their child and working actively for the child's maximum potential development (Crawford, 1979).

Inherent in the family systems view of working with parents is the notion that dysfunctional system is distinguished by its rigidity and resistance to change. On the other hand, healthy systems are flexible and open to change (Hackney, 1981).

As professionals we must assume that parents:

1. are interested in the growth of their child and would like to improve their interaction with him.

2. can be helped to improve the skills necessary for interaction.

3. can work in a classroom setting, including one in which their own child is participating.

4. will find the time to become involved if the involvement is meaningful.

5. will learn most effectively when their training is specific and has direct application.

6. are easiest to involve when their goals and values are congruent with those of the school and most difficult when there is a great discrepancy in the "match."

7. will require the greatest flexibility in programming when there is a wide discrepancy in the "match."

8. will become involved to the extent they participate in decision making.

9. will involve themselves most when feedback exists and is positive.

10. will involve themselves most when professional personnel show a genuine respect for the family members as individuals.

11. will involve themselves most when served by professional personnel who have been trained to work with family members in divergent appropriate ways.

12. will involve themselves most when the approach is highly individualized.

13. will be able to apply new knowledge to other family members, particularly other children.

14. will develop more positive attitudes when the involvement is successful.

15. will need less help and support from professional staff as they acquire more effective knowledge and skills.

16. may acquire sufficient skills to work with family members of other families.

The above set of assumptions should help clarify the basis on which working relationships might be established. Implementation of these ideas may be difficult because of the breadth of the assumptions and the magnitude of problems (Karens et. al. 1972).

Most recently, professionals have looked to the theoretical family systems approach to working with families with disabled members. According to Turnbull et. al. (1983) the family systems approach takes the position that the consumer is the whole family. This rationale is predicated on the fact that all the family members affected by the disability must be given attention and that the disabled individual can be assisted through the family. This model assumes that each family is unique, that the interaction within each family is contantly changing and has varying boundaries, that each family fulfills a variety of functions, and that changes produce varied degrees of stress for all family members. The components of this model are as follows:

1. Family structure consists of the descriptive characteristics of the family, including the nature of its membership and its cultural and ideological style. These characteristics are the *input* into the interactional system— the resources, the perception of the world— that shape the way in which the family interacts.

2. Family interaction is the hub of the system, the process of interaction among family members. Input into the system (structure) has determined the rules by which the family is governed as it interacts: its level of cohesion, its adaptability, and its communicatin style. Finally, these interactions work together to serve individual member and collective family needs.

3. Family function is the output of the interactional system. Utilizing the resources available through its structure (input) the family interacts (proceses) to produce responses that fulfill nine major categories of need.

4. Family life cycle introduces the element of change into the family system. As the family moves through time, developmental and nondevelopmental changes alter the family structure and/or the family's needs. These, in turn, produce change in the way the family interacts (Turnbull et. al., 1983).

Schilling et al., (1984) summarize the trends when they state: "Social supports enable parents to maintain a sense of normalcy, and give them strength when their personal coping ability ebbs. . . and social supports are teachable helping strategies. With institutionalized social services decreasing, parents of handicapped children may profit from increased personal coping skills and greater participation in social support systems. Family practitioners using this approach have programmatic and powerful methods to better serve a challenging client group" (p. 52).

Longo and Bond (1984) speak to the issue of families that are stressed but coping well and in view of this, several outcomes could be very useful. For example, a parenting framework for assessment and intervention could be better explained to parents, and approaches successfully used by parents should be identified and shared, thus facilitating more positive attitudinal and practice models. And according to other theorists, mothers of handicapped children in the early months are much like mothers of normal babies, and this mainstreaming of mothers should occur during these months (Busch-Rossnagel et al., 1984).

Family systems theories appear to hold the most promise for serving special children and their families.

Application Activities

1. Interview at least three parents of handicapped or gifted children regarding their use of community resources. Include such questions as which resources they use frequently and infrequently, why they make use of some resources and not others, and who they trust/mistrust.

2. Survey your community. Make a list of facilitators as well as barriers to parent education for the "special needs" child.

3. Survey *TV Guide* for programs on gifted and/or handicapped. Make a

list of programs that provide assistance or resources to parents and parenting.

4. Make a list of at least five rules for a child seven years old with a special problem. Describe how you went about making these rules and develop a list of recommendations for implementation.

5. Obtain a current issue of a parent magazine. Make a list of the topics suitable for parents of "special children." Write a brief summary of one of the articles.

6. Identify a topic for research in the field of parent education and "special children." Read and write a brief summary of a research articles pertaining to the topic.

7. Interview a family life educator, parent educator, or a professor of child development on parent counseling approaches and special techniques they find most useful.

8. Create a "model" education program for parents of "special" children. Include such aspects as:
   1. what material would be presented
   2. how that material would be presented
   3. how the program would be promoted
   4. methods for feedback/evaluation

9. Identify barriers to parent education and programs for special children in your community. Describe ways in which these barriers might be overcome.

10. The media can be used as an avenue to present and/or promote parent education. Compose a letter to the editor advocating one aspect of parent education and training for special children. Submit it for publication.

11. Write a child-care article for submission to a parent' magazine. Be sure to consider such aspects as writing for the lay audience and focusing on a particular condition.

12. Write a proposal for a parent education/special education research project.

13. Interview the coordinator or an established parent education program and focus on the evaluation aspect of the program.

Bibliography

Bricklin, P.M. 1970. Counseling parents of children with learning disabilities. *The Reading Teacher,* 1: 23:4: 331 – 338.

Briston, M.W. 1984. The birth of a handicapped child— a wholistic model for grieving. *Family Relations,* 33 (1): 25 – 39.

Busch-Rossnagel, N.A., D.L. Peters and M.J. Daly. 1984. Mothers of vulnerable and normal infants: more alike than different. *Family Relations,* 33 (1): 57 – 65.

Crawford, L. 1979. Parent potential. *Volta Review,* 81: 514 – 16.

Colangelo, N. and D.F. Dettmann. 1980. A functional model for counseling parents of gifted students. *Gifted Child Quarterly,* 24 (4): 158 – 61.

Drotar, E. et. al. 1975. The adoption of parents at the birth of an infant with a congential malformation: a hypothetical model. *Pediatrics,* 11: 56: 5, 710 – 716.

Fanning, P. 1977. New relationships between parents and schools. *Focus on Exceptional Children,* 9: 1 – 12.

Gallagher, J.J. 1975. *Teaching the Gifted Chld,* 2nd edition. Allyn Bacon, Inc., Boston, MS.

Goldson, E. 1979. Parents' reactions to the birth of a sick infant. *Children Today,* 8: 13 – 17.

Greene, L. 1983. *Kids Who Hate School.* Atlanta: Humanics Limited.

Hackney, H. 1981. Adrift in the mainstream. *The Exceptional Parent,* 9: E3 – E6.

Hanley, M.R. 1979. Adrift in the mainstream. *The Exceptional Parent.* 9: 3 – 6.

Heisler, V. 1972. *A Handicapped Child in the Family: A Guide For Parents.* New York: Gurne and Stratton.

Karens, M., R. Zehrback, and J.A. Teska. 1972. Involving families of handicapped children. *Parents are Teachers: Theory Into Practice,* 11: 150 – 56.

Kaplan, D.M. and E. A. Mason. 1960. Maternal reactions to premature birth viewed as an acute emotional disorder. *American Journal of Orthopsychiatry,* 30 (3): 539 – 552.

Longo, D.C. and L. Bond. 1984. Families of the handicapped child: research and practice. *Family Relations,* 33 (1): 57 – 65.

Love, H. 1970. *Parental Attitudes Toward Exceptional Children.* Charles C. Thomas: Springfield, Illinois.

Loveless, S.C. 1981. CDA: Children with special needs. Oscar Rose Junior

College, 6420 Southeast 15 th, Midwest City, Oklahoma, 73110.

Peters, N.A. and W.T. Stephenson, Jr. 1979. Parents as partners in a program for children with oral language and reading disabilities. *Teaching Exceptional Children,* 11: 64 – 66.

Ross, A.O. 1964. *The Exceptional Child in the Family.* Grune and Stratton: New York.

Rotter, J.C. and E.H. Robinson, III. 1982. *Parent- Teachers Conferencing.* NEA Publication, Washington, D.C.

Schilling. R.F. et. al. 1984. Coping and social support in families of developmentally disabled children. *Family Relations,* 33 (1): 47 – 54.

Turnbull, A.P. et. al. 1983. *Working With Families With Disabled Members: A Family Systems Approach.* University of Kansas Research and Training Center on Independent Living. University of Kansas, Lawrence, Kansas. 66045.

United States Department of Health, Education and Welfare. 1975. *The Problems of Mental Retardation.* Government Publications, Washington, D.C.

United States Department of Health, Education and Welfare. Standards for Special Education, State Department of Education, Columbus, Ohio.

United State Department of Health, Education and Welfare. 1977. Diagram Group *Child's Body a Parent's Manual.* Paddington Press Ltd. (Distributed by Grosset and Dunlap). New York.

8. The "New School" Family Life Model

Generalization

Society has become increasingly aware of the problems and responsibilities of parents who are not adequately prepared to establish a positive family environment. As a result, elementary schools should consider the purpose and function of helping parents successfully manage their lives and their children's. Particularly, this plan would establish a Family Life Center in every neighborhood elementary school. The program would be one that would conduct training and home visits and share appropriate information relative to needs assessment findings in all aspects of family life and as applied to all preschool children. Family Life Centers would focus on elements with which families must deal and strive to give parents the insight necessary to raise healthy, happy children.

The rationale for this plan is the fact that education is preventive whereas other support systems (that is, welfare and hospitals) are remedial. Elementary schools exist in every neighborhood, and this setting will allow families to identify with the "process of education" in a positive developmental way. Their children will eventually attend the respective neighborhood schools. What better way to build for the future than to develop a strong reciprocal relationship between parents and education?

Educational systems would assume this role in the preschool years, not only for parents of four and five year olds, but in other ways for the three, two, and one year olds and, in fact, all the way back to birth and prenatal development (White, 1967).

If education is to meet more of the society's needs, one of the best changes would be to add well-trained human development specialists to the elementary school staff to promote healthy families. A system such as this one does not exist at this time. Since the American family is in transition, parents are asking for help (Miles, 1977). Schools are in a strategic social position and could be a most appropriate answer to the serious national social problem — that of reinforcing the positive nature and function of the family.

Objectives

1. To present a rationalization for a hypothetical model of a New School parent education program

2. To review and identify training content and variable trends useful for planning and evaluating professional programs

3. To present a review of the effectiveness of various educational programs designed for parents

4. To rationalize the need for a closer relationship between parents and public elementary schools and the need to establish Family Life programs for families served by neighborhood schools

5. To suggest future directions for parent education programs in schools

The "New School"

What seems to be emerging in the early intervention field is a strong interest in, if not a trend toward, indirect intervention through parent education. What is needed is a consistent, dependable, ensured arrangement for reaching all parents, particularly new families that are having first and second children.

The neighborhood elementary school would be a likely institution for such outreach. It already serves a specific population and each school in each community could provide the added function and implementation of a Family Life component. Trained family life workers would be added to the elementary school staff. Their main task would be to design a family life program that would meet the needs of the population served by that elementary school. For example, some neighborhoods may consist of working mothers, some of low-income parents, and some of single family parents. Each would require special considerations.

Besides the benefit of serving unique community needs, this "new school" model could provide an in-take screening function. It is not necessary to wait until a child is seven or eight years old to discover he has learning or behavior problems. Society can assume a more pro-health and preventive approach to family life. The professional family life or human development specialist could coordinate a multidisciplinary team including medical and speech and hearing personnel to arrange screening and follow-uyp services. Other team members could make home visits as well as plan and arrange for in-school child care and parent training pertinent to child development concepts. Family life variables of management, nutrition, and community participation can be encouraged.

An additional benefit would be the more efficient use of physical facilities and the coordination of transition into regular elementary school. Understandably, the major gain will be the promotion of healthier families. Education needs innovation and families ned help. The match is a natural one.

The interconnections, implemented through the "new school" elementary concepts, are shown in Figure 2.

According to Powell (1979) significant elements are program implementation and maintenance, interactions, and change characteristics. The "new school" model would necessarily include these concepts and the concepts illustrated in Figure 3.

Topics and Techniques

Although parent education covers a range of topics and techniques, a distinction can be made between two types of educational efforts. One type is based on information and is an attempt to provide parents with useful information. This could include information about safety, health facts and resources, and nutrition information.

Another type is an effort to assist parents in developing positive and appropriate child-rearing practices. Examples are instruction in methods of discipline,
advice on how to deal with aggression or hostility, methods for handling
extreme expressions of emotion, and warnings about the consequences of
rejection or neglect. This instruction involves the parents' ability to nurture,
teach, discipline, and interact with their children.

If it is to address interactional processes, parent education will also attempt
to change established patterns of interpersonal behavior and to help the parent
to be more effective in caring for his child. The challenge to the school is to
broaden its traditional area of service and to become an extended family. To
focus narrowly on cognitive skills is no longer enough, if it ever was enough.
A truly basic approach to education involves the recognition of the wholeness
of a child's being in the context of his family and community (Gross, 1977).

The System

The educational system has shown a remarkable resistance to change.
School routines, practices, and outcomes do not easily budge, either for good
ideas or bad ideas. If problems diminish in a particular school, the reduction
is more often due to the outside events than to in-school programs. Part of
the reason schools are so poor at solving social problems is the general
impotence or overrated importance of most school experiences. Schools can
make a difference. They usually reinforce economic, social, and personal
factors; they should be able to reinforce the variables that will strengthen
"family life."

The Content

In general, parent education classes should provide a supportive, nonjudg-
mental environment in which parents feel free to investigate and discuss
creative options for assisting with their child's social, emotional, and physical
growth. While the participants should receive information on child growth
and development, the personal growth of each parent also should be empha-
sized. Parents should be encouraged to recognize their own responsibility and
individual strength for promoting optimal growth in their child. They should
be encouraged to develop ideas and techniques that will stimulate the child's
physical, emotional, social, and academic development.

Based on knowledge of growth patterns and a sensitivity to each child's
uniqueness, parent education classes should assist parents to set realistic
expectations for their child. They should provide opportunities for sharing
and appreciating the different cultural values held by various ethnic groups in

the community. Parents should be provided with an opportunity, through the classes, to practice a broad variety of skills in communications, problem-solving, and other areas that may enhance family relations. Additionally, classes should assist parents in dealing effectively with school-parent concerns so as to promote maximum learning. Criteria for organizing programs (Brim, 1959) should generally include well defined and measurable objectives, strategies that will appeal to adults, curriculum that is relevant for the groups being served, continuity through documentation, assessment and evaluation.

Forms and Methods

Parent education classes can be presented in a variety of forms. Brim (1959) discusses the influence of parental ability factors such as intelligence, energy levels, unconscious factors, culture values, social behavior, group structures, and ecological or physical factors. He explains how these influence the content of a training program.

Successful parent education classes can generally include:

1. parent participation in which parents, with supervision, work directly with children in the classroom under guidance of a skilled teacher. These may be paid or volunteer.

2. discussion groups or informative meetings based on needed content and designed along adult education principles.

3. film series or book reviews as the basis for class content.

4. classes or open meetings designed to acquaint community members with the goals and procedures of school programs.

5. child observation followed by guided parent discussions.

6. classes for parents of special children.

7. combined parent-teacher workshops.

8. outdoor education emphasizing living, learning, and playing together.

Administrative and staff attitudes are crucial to successful parent involvement and must reflect a genuine interest in and support of both parent education and parent participation. Some practical suggestions could include:

1. work with school administrators, staff, teachers, auxiliary and resource people to facilitate maximum effectiveness.

2. interpret to teachers how parent education classes can be supportive.

3. enlist enthusiastic school personnel as teachers for the program.

4. use community agencies to help meet the total needs of the parents who attend.

5. create a place for parents at the school through a "parent room". Hold all classes or meetings in a convenient place.

6. encourage parents to serve on policy making and advisory committees.

7. arrange some social activities in which positive communication can take place.

8. conduct surveys to discover what classes would be interesting to parents and what times would be convenient.

9. make sure that course titles are interesting and clearly describe course contents. Attach an outline of staff skills and talents.

10. design and distribute attractive flyers, announcements, and brochures for classes at churches, supermarkets, and other public buildings.

11. fnd out what other successful programs have been doing.

12. disseminate information through news media— television, radio and newspapers.

Parent-Professional Interaction and Obstacles

In a sense, programs and materials designed for parents create a parasocial relationship between parents and professionals, even though there is no direct personal contact between them. In this relationship parents are clearly amateurs. The prestige of the professional is very high and is often further bolstered by his institutional base such as a clinic, a school, a day-care center, a welfare agency, a probation department, a community agency, or a university. If not properly planned and managed, parent education programs can give parents feelings of powerlessness and dependence on the advice of professionals. In fact, Brim (1959) describes this as a potential conflict between the values of parents and educators.

Some individuals and families hesitate to enroll in programs because they are concerned about being labeled. They may also fear that, by enrolling, they may discover they are not as effective a family member as they had thought. Other families think they can deal with problems or crises on their own.

Many agencies that plan and sponsor Family Life programs tend to be influenced by the anticipated community resistance. This resistance tends to ignore the obvious need of families to enhance their strengths and problem-solving abilities. Consequently, when there is no immediate and enthusiastic community response, the programs are often discontinued. Schools should expect communities to resist the concept of Family Lfe for many reasons, yet officials should not write off the community as indifferent. Even with resistance the community can benefit from the program, especially if it is adequately prepared.

The premium that parents place on school life is a self-fulfilling prophecy well demonstrated through children's achievements. When a teacher lets a parent see that he or she is considered a contributing partner in his or her child's learning, the expectation tends to become a reality. The parents and schools join to work toward a common goal. Here, learning is viewed as an active, not a passive, process group facilitator. The "new school" can help foster self-confidence, self-respect, assertiveness, and group interaction skills; it can also help maintain a high level of involvement in children's school experiences. Further benefits include greater community awareness of school-related issues (Guttman, 1978).

The New School Variables

The "new school" Family Life model, in addition to training parents, would serve as the curriculum development and resource center for the families whose children attend each respective elementary school.

In the 1980s there will be more specialists at all levels of education, and in particular counseling programs at the elementary level, will increase. As a result, a shortage of trained professionals may develop, creating a need for more educators to enter this field. These general education needs can be translated to a concurrent need for "parent" educators.

School Change

How can schools reshape to meet family life needs? It may be advantageous to begin with the inclusion of a professional Family Life educator in the elementary environment. In the Family Life approach, one is trusting the school environment to be innovative and in each case it is assumed there is motivation and a capacity for serving families. However, the variables in the family life teaching-learning settings are too complex to be predicted and controlled by any standard curriculum. Each family life program will evolve its own curriculum, in content and sequence or both, as the nature of the participants is considered.

New Teachers for New Needs

Most import is the need for educators who can function broadly, not only as teachers of facts and skills, but as team workers concerned with total development. If elementary schools are to be comprehensive centers of family development, practitioners need to recognize the ways in which their disciplines overlap. Teachers specialize in learning and cognition, nurses specialize in health, psychologists specialize in mental health, and social workers specialize in community life, but all are involved with the totality of a person as he or she copes with the challenges of the "new school."

The responsible parent educator does not have a series of answers readily available for the inquiring parent. He or she is not equipped with a set of lesson plans that will serve as a blueprint for parents. While the parent educator may be an "expert" in one or more fields pertinent to the parent-child relationship, he or she is not a scientific technician who can furnish specific formulas for the solution of parents' problems. Rather, the family life specialist helps parents incorporate and use theories and practices that apply to their specific situations.

Family Life coordinaters can work with the area schools in a number of different ways. By meeting with kindergarten teachers, principals, and administrators, they help school representatives become more familiar with family life concepts and at the same time help school staff learn more about Family Life policies and procedures. Family Life coordinators work toward coordination of services for the mutual benefit of schools, children, and families. Some of the tasks that a Family Life coordinator might undertake are:

1. conduct kindergarten visits and coordination of enrollment

2. plan and conduct annual training meetings

3. refer families who wish to enroll or who need other community services

4. conduct round-ups for health screening and other special events

5. transmit information

6. train parents

7. plan social events for both parents and school personnel

8. make home visits for recruitment and education purposes

9. coordinate with teachers, principals, and superintendent

10. advocate parent education programs

11. link special services (handicapped, gifted)

12. conduct needs assessment, plans, and evaluation (Burke, 1981)

Trained Family Life Educators

Brim (1959) suggests that professional parent educators can be specially trained from within the following disciplines:

1. professionals trained in Family Life Educators baccalaureate programs

2. clinical personnel: psychiatrists, clinical psychologists, and social workers

3. home economics, human development, or family specialists

4. teachers (general)

5. medical personnel

6. nurses

7. clergymen and religious educators

8. parents

Family life is a many-faceted and parent-child relations involve a great variety of factors. Consequently, the parent educator, if he is to serve as a consultant, guide, and resource person, must have a broad grounding in those things which have an impact on the family and which can contribute to its welfare. In a sense, this educator serves as a middleman between the specialized expert and family members and therefore must be acquainted with the findings of psychologists, physicians, psychiatrists, sociologists, economists, and anthropologists.

Professional Expertise
The deep personal and professional satisfactions that come from work with parents are bringing increasing numbers of workers from many backgrounds into the parent education circle. It may well be that this movement, which

originated in the United States, is becoming one of the most challenging and creative education endeavors of the country.

Further, the experienced parent educator does not assume that most parents are inept, ignorant, or lacking the desire to do the best possible job as parents. The past twenty years may reflect the increase in the number of professionals in specialities oriented toward families.

Professional groups draw their advice for parents from research and clinical experience, both of which have high prestige in the community. This prestige is bolstered by credentials, licensees, certificates, and diplomas, and by state laws that prohibit counseling without proper certification.

Need for Specialists

Gross (1977) explains that the number of children under six living in single parent homes is rapidly increasing. Further, the number of working mothers in increasing, as is the number of children born to adolescent mothers. These facts should be considered as evidence for the need for more Family Life education. The times have changed and systems of support must change with them. The question is this: Will schools attempt to fill the void created by the changing family?

Mass change is needed and the "new school" could be the answer. It could provide the power to produce real change in educational quality and service.

Funding Sources

Extensive preplanning, commitment from community schools, and willing students are essential ingredients for the success of the "new school." This includes funding. Funding models could take a number of different directions.

For example, the Home Economics section of the Arizona Department of Education has promoted multiple funding sources for their programs. Another model has been the federal vocational funds for the consumer and homemaking. School districts and related service agencies can contribute valuable "inkind" resources such as transportation, building space, resource personnel, and technical assistance. Love (1979) mentions using adult education resources, special funds, district cooperatives, and private funds.

Exactly how far to go in terms of dollars per year, of course, is not fully agreed upon. An expenditure of perhaps $300 or $400 per year per family probably could facilitate screening and basic concept education. It is difficult to think of a better way to spend that money than to invest in improving the quality of our early educational systems (Irvine et al., 1979).

When soliciting funds, it is necessary to be aware of the range of community reactions to the program and the reasons for the reactions. "Family Life Education" is, unfortunately, a poorly understood concept to many professionals and in many communities. Even after years of publicity and explanation, the definition is confusing. This confusion is compounded when different agencies label their preventive education services "life enrichment" or "family development programs." The phrase "Family Life Education" is used only by professionals and is seldom heard of in the community.

Program Effectiveness

Several studies have reported increases in the factual knowledge of parents who have participated in parent education programs. Endres and Evans (1968) evaluated a community education project in parent-child relations and concluded that the attitudes of parents who attended discussion groups showed significant improvement over those of the control group.

Formal evaluation and basic experimental research in parent education demand the best criteria. There is clear evidence from this study that children of parents who enrolled in parent education programs showed greater acceptance of themselves. Nevertheless, more experimental studies are needed to find out whether certain programs are more effective than others and certain methods are better than others in bringing about positive behavior change (Endres and Evans, 1968).

Evaluation has come late to the field of parent education, and much that has been done has been criticized as unsound since the evaluation attempts have relied heavily on participant assessment rather than on observations and reports of unbiased and uninvolved observers. Direct and extensive observation of parent-child interaction in real-life situations would probably yield the most valid data for a study of this kind. However, the difficulty and expense of collecting such data forces the research worker to rely on structured interviews and objective attitude inventories.

According to Wilson (1979), parent training needs closer examination from at least three perspectives:

1. Research needs to confirm the efficacy of parent training programs based on specified gains measured in the parents' children. To demonstrate that a parent has learned some skills in behavioral management does not allow us to conclude the child has benefited from the parent's skill.

2. Parent trainers need to know what information and skills are important to parents on a selective basis. For instance, trainers need to know which

parent needs behavioral skills, which parent needs to develop more effective communication with his child, and which parent needs developmental knowledge to better understand his child's behavior. Parents cannot simply be randomly trained in whatever skill is popular with the trainer.

3. Related to this is the need for a comparison of current training programs from which an individual can intelligently select. This would include a list of the goals of each type of training and some suggestions about characteristics of the parent and child who may benefit by such training.

Some new measurement techniques go beyond the unimaginative and often even thoughtless use in the past of intelligence test scores and standard achievement test scores as yardsticks of program effectiveness. If the measurement of program effects should include attention to children's social-emotional progress, then child measures must address this issue by looking at the coping/noncoping distinction and at psycho-social maturity.

Other processes which need evaluation are the ways in which the program adapts to and accommodates the subculture of its community. The degree to which the parent education enhances or disrupts the transmission of cultural characteristics through parent-child relations is a crucial issue. Secondly, the professional socialization of program staff and the roles they assume are also important, especially those of paraprofessional workers. The issues here are professional identity, staff-family boundaries, and the interpersonal skills required of paraprofessionals working with small groups of parents.

A third dimension of program refinement and maintenance is the relationship to existing education and human services in the community, including various operations of the project's co-sponsoring public school. Parent education provides a potentially competitive entry into the territorial network of human services offered by public and private nonschool agencies. A program dealing with the social milieu of parents can be expected to infringe upon child and family services provided by other human service agencies. A related issue is the degree to which this program becomes institutionalized into the basic operation of its co-sponsoring agencies. Powell (1978) continues to point out that the overall aim is to define and describe operational components of the program and to analyze the development and nature of interpersonal relationships associated with each component.

Other indices of program effectiveness and individual differences among parents that can be evaluated are parental social networks (kin, friend, and neighbor interaction), life events stress, everyday family coping, parent help-seeking behaviors surrounding child care issues, maternal childrearing atti-

tudes, and mother-infant interaction (Powell, 1979). One additional approach
to evaluation assumes that the program and the families it serves are independent social systems with their own properties, values, and modes of operations
and that the problems arise when systems conflict or intersect.

Research and evaluation generally have neglected the issue of how programs actually function. Parents approach intervention programs with differing
needs, stresses, and existing resources. Little is known about the influence of
parent attributes and family circumstances on program effectiveness. Program
staff, for example, cannot be expected to be uniformly enthusiastic, energetic,
and perceptive with each parent (Powell, 1975).

Perhaps the most significant limitation of current process evaluation work
is a conceptual one. Process evaluators seek to determine whether the program
has been directed at the appropriate target population and whether the intervention efforts have been carried out as specified in the program design or
derived from principles explicated in the design. While these are important
functions of process evaluation, it could be argued that process evaluation
can play a potentially significant role in uncovering the determinants of program effectiveness. The measurement of program processes can yield insight
into the social processes affecting program operations and the interconnections
between specific program properties and the outcomes of participants.

Future Directions

At present, there is only limited literature to point out those characteristics
that would indicate the appropriateness of one type of parental involvement
over another. Research should include effort to identify those characteristics.

Programs for parents tend to be random with little assessment of the
parent-child need as an aid to effective and efficient planning. Future programs should demonstrate their efficacy as well as their relevance for the
particular parent-child need (Wilson, 1979). Another approach to parent
education might also take more seriously the established principle that learner
initiative is a crucial element in the development of a new skill.

Structured programs for parent education in the elementary schools can
readily serve as appropriate research ground. Public school boundaries are
established and familiar. The attendance area is a basic unit that is close to
parent and families; it is a unit in which people know one another and in
which mutual interests and concerns encourage cooperation. It is large enough
to provide a variety of services efficiently, yet small enough to provide a
sense of community.

Secondly, the author agrees with Hughes (1979) when he suggests that the foremost national organization devoted to parent education— the PTA— could be a research resource. In all parts of the country, PTAs are already organized and functioning in the local communities.

The empirical evidence is far from conclusive in identifying approaches that are most effective for working with parents in early childhood intervention efforts. It appears that those programs which are highly structured, involve parents for extended time periods, employ goal-specific curricula, and contain projects planned and carried out by parents themselves are likely to have importance for parents and their children (Gordon, 1979).

Hughes (1979) suggests the following as potential methods for implementing a comprehensive program of parent and family education:

1. integrate family and parent education studies into all levels of the public school curriculum

2. explore the feasibility of requiring or encouraging premarriage counseling for very young couples

3. seek funds and support for permanent interdisciplinary institutes dedicated to the study of children and families

4. develop community-based early childhood and family education programs that stress parental participation

5. incorporate the functions of PTA groups into these new early childhood/ parent education programs

6. consider the feasibility of providing a tax credit or some other incentive to all parents who actively participate

Our goal must be to help parents maintain a sense of power, dignity, and authority in the rearing of their children. This is what parent education is all about. If parents have the power to do so, most of them will accept the long-term responsibility of caring for and supporting their children. By eliminating factors that undercut family life and make it hard for parents to function as parents, we will create an environnment in which parents can do a truly responsible job of raising children (Hughes, 1979).

New School Outcomes

Although the organizational difficulties are serious, it would be worthwhile to examine the effectiveness of such concepts as the "new school" elementary model and to develop programs useful to parents who wish to organize their own groups.

If these new models are successful, the impact will extend beyond the local community. According to Van Zijdevild (1976) the new model in a community can be expected to:

1. influence national education policy toward an increased concern for the earliest years of life

2. serve as a model for other communities who wish to start early childhood programs

3. change the distribution of resources within school systems by increasing funds for the preschool year

4. draw the family, schools, and medical profession into a relation of shared responsibility for the early development of the child

5. shift the orientation of school and community health services toward prevention rather than remediation

6. influence training of pediatricians not only by extending the range of their diagnostic tools, but also by preparing them to recognize indications of potential educational handicaps

7. influence training of teachers, paraprofessionals, and parents to respond to the needs and interests of young children and to help them grow in competence and confidence.

8. affect space usage in schools currently undergoing architectural planning, paying special note to health, pupil personnel services, and play area allocations

9. demonstrate the utility of a cost-effectiveness approach in educational evaluation

10. influence instructional efforts of the school more toward the child's developmental level of functioning, gradually minimizing and eliminating "grade readiness"

11. enhance the recent efforts of state and federal legislators toward increased integration of handicapped children into regular school programs

12. encourage substantial movement of parents and the medical community into the school, necessitating modification of staff attitudes and retraining of teachers, administrators, and pupil personnel staff

Each elementary school could include a range of programs, depending again on the nature of the population being served. Gross (1977) suggests a number of very appropriate activities:

1. indoor-outdoor education and recreation for children ages 0 to eight

2. early morning and late afternoon day-care

3. adult classes and recreational activities

4. tutoring and homework help for children

5. a crafts center for creating learning materials

6. discussion and support groups for parents

7. child development information

8. a health and nutrition center for basic screening examinations, inoculations, and access to health resources

9. leadership development

10. seminars on community issues

11. a center for an evening and weekend emergency "hot line"

12. special supports and classes for pregnant girls, adolescent parents, and young families

13. availability of breakfast and lunch

14. a swap center for outgrown clothing

15. opportunities for community volunteers to teach and demonstrate skills

16. summer activities for families

A systematic cycle can be enormously helpful in reviewing plans for a parent education program. The phases to this cycle include:
assessment (learn as much as you can about existing needs, materials, amounts of time, and so on), *development* (utilize your most effective staff, parents, and other citizens to determine standards and guidelines), implementation (once a district-wide thrust has been agreed upon, begin implementation of the program), *evaluation* (set up the design for evaluation at the beginning; evaluation goes hand in hand with needs assessment), and *feedback/modification* (utilizing what we know and discovering major weaknesses; specialists and others ought to have a system for determining and disseminating those components that work). (Love, 1979.)

Potential Barriers

There is a sense within this country that families, schools, and communities are expressing both a need for and a receptivity to parent education, but what are the barriers to implementation? Which are real barriers, and which are not? We can classify the barriers as political, financial, technical, communicative, or social.

As in every area of social policy, politics is crucial. Local public schools may wish to be responsive to the parent education needs of their patrons, but if legislative, administrative, organizational, or financial barriers cannot be overcome, schools will give up before they begin. Even if laws and regulations allow and encourage parent involvement and education, there must be district and building administrative support. If we educate teachers and parent educators, we must also educate principals and superintendentsn many cases the most difficult barrier will be financial, not because resources are unavailable, but because priorities are elsewhere.

Barriers also include a lack of trained, experienced personnel and a lack of materials and methods appropriate for families, particularly those with pre-school and elementary-school-age children. Furthermore, there are communication barriers among the agencies, institutions, and groups involved in parent education. Although it is true that the familiar territorial impulse is heightened by scarce resources, school involvement in parent education is unlikely to lessen the need for family education services from any of these other groups.

Barriers relating to social values have never been very honestly confronted in parent education. We have to face the fact that there is no such thing as the ideal parent in any culture. If we can adjust to this idea, then some of the barriers may be overcome— and many will prove to be nonexistent. Potential barriers may not totally disappear but they certainly can be overcome, particularly if mandates, rigidity, and narrow conceptions of parent education are avoided (McAfee, 1979).

Voluntary parent education programs, designed with the help of parents to meet the needs of today's parents, can enhance any program that works with children, whether those are young children in a preprimary program or adolescents who are themselves preparing to be parents.

The age of parental involvement has arrived— if schools utilize some of the ideals and philosophies of Family Life Education as explained and described, children, families and communities will reap the benefits.

Application Activities

1. Observe or interview parent education program directors. Classify positive and negative observations as they relate to program design, curricular and goals.

2. Develop a "parent handout" on a given topic.

3. Develop a "needs assessment" instrument and submit it to a minimum of fifty parents as a model program planning strategy.

4. Design and/or conduct a research study relating to one issue.

5. Visit an exemplary Family Life model and synthesize the factors and issues which emerge as most important.

6. Interview twenty-six parents for the purpose of ascertaining their attitudes about:
   • early screening
   • training content needs
   • acceptance of schools as a helping agent
   • themselves as educators

7. Review, analyze, and compare four teacher-training curricula in regard to preparation of Family Life Education.

8. Examine elements of social service support systems in your home community. Analyze the team effort among these services.

9. Examine one system (for example, a health clinic), and analyze the team efforts within this system.

10. Design an innovative model of a comprehensive "new school" Family Life model. Include cooperating agencies, a curriculum model, funding, and staffing patterns.

Bibliography

Brim, O.G. 11959. *Education for Child Rearing*. Russell Sage Foundation.

Burke, P. 1981. Home/school linkage model comprehensive exam project. Master of Education Project, Home Economics Department, Bowling Green State University 43402.

Endres, M.P., and M.J. Evans. 1968. Some effects of parent education on parents and their children. *Adult Education Journal*, 18: 101 – 111.

Euchner, Charlie. 1983. New York considers enrolling students at age four. *Education Week*, Box 1983, Marion, Ohio 43305, Vol. 2:19.

Gordon, I., et. al. 1979. How has follow-through promoted parent involvement? *Young Children*, Vol. 34: 49 – 53.

Gross, D.W. 1977. Improving the quality of family life. *Childhood Education*, Vol. 54; No. 2, pp. 50 – 54.

Guttman, J. 1978. Getting parents involved in preschool. *The Education Digest*, Vol. 44, pp. 15 – 17.

Hughes, J.M. 1979. A Commitment to Parent Education. Education Commission of the States. Report # 121. Suite 200, 1860 Lincoln St., Denver, Colorado. January. pp. 6 – 9.

Hoffert, L., et al. 1979. Simulation workshop for parents evoking empathic responses. *Academic Therapy*, Vol. 15, pp. 5 – 11.

Irvine, David J., et. al. 1979. Parent Involvement Affects Children's Cognitive Growth. The University of the State of New York. The State Education Department. Division of Research. Prekindergarten Evaluation Unit. Albany, New York 12234. August 31.

Love, R. 1979. Parents and Public Schools. Partners in Education. *Implementing Parent Education*. Education Commission of the States Report #121. Suite 300, 1860 Lincoln Street, Denver, Colorado. January. pp. 23 – 26.

McAfee, O. 1979. Parent Education: Needed Characteristics and Necessary Concerns. *Implementing Parent Education*. Education Commission of the States. Report #121. Suite 300, 1860 Lincoln Street, Denver, Colorado. pp. 37 – 41.

Miles, C.G. 1977. Helping parents help their children. *The Education Digest*, Vol. 43: 57 – 59.

Powell, D.R. 1979. Social interaction approval to parent education: An overview of the child and family neighborhood program. The Merrill Palmer Institute, 71 E. Ferry Avenue, Detroit, Michigan 48208.

Schaefer, E.S. 1979. Professionals and parents: Moving toward partnership.

Keynote address given at the 1979 Parenting Conference, 25 April, 1979, at Virginia Commonwealth University, Richmond, Virginia.

Van Zijderveld, B. 1976. Early stimulation programs for young severely retarded children. *Research Exchange and Practice in Mental Reatardation,* Vol. 2: 54 – 60.

Weikart, D. 1971. *Early childhood special education for intellectually subnormal and/or culturally different children.* Ypsilanti, Michigan: HiScope Educational Research Roundation.

White, B.L. 1967. Pre-school education, a plea for common sense. Paper presented at the Annual meeting of the National Association of Independent Schools, 4 March 1967 in New York City, pp. 1 – 10.

Wilson, W. 1979. Parent training: Some observations. *Academic Therapy, Vol. 15: 45 – 51.*

Zigler, E.F. 1978. America's head start program: An agenda for its second decade. *Young Children,* Vol. 33: 6, 4 – 11.

Annotated List of Resources

These resource references were chosen because they offer relatively inexpensive or free "parent education" materials.

Printed:

1. Public Affairs Committee, Inc.
   381 Park Avenue
   New York, New York 10016

Appropriate parent education pamphlets on various topics for parents and professionals.

2. The Center for Parent Education
   55 Chapel Street
   Newton, Massachusetts 02160

Materials for Education for Parenthood activities: consultations on research and service programs, professional training institutes and workshops, audiovisual materials and staff training and parents, personnel guidance, research projects and conference presentations.

3. Parenting in 1977: A Listing of Parenting Materials
   Division of Community and Family Education
   Southwest Educational Development Laboratory
   211 East 7th Street
   Austin, Texas 78701

A significant collection of appropriate materials for a variety of parent education topics.

4. J.C. Penney, Inc.
   Consumer Affairs Department
   1301 Avenue of the Americas
   New York, New York 10019

A collection of leaflets and bulletins focused on family or parent topics.

5. Resource Lists of Parenting, Socialization, Discipline and Family Living and other related Topics, Children's Rights and Advocacy Television for Children, etc.
   ERIC-ECE
   805 W. Pennsylvania Avenue
   Urbana, Illinois 61801

A listing of specific parenting professional or academic references.

6. Center for Human Services
   2084 Cornell Road
   Cleveland, Ohio 44106

Reference that deals with the organizational structure of parent co-op groups, roles of parents and techers, purposed and methods of parent education, and policies and procedures for running a business.

7. Everyone Needs a Parent
   Western Federation for
   Human Services
   145 – 4th Avenue, Suite #615
   Seattle, Washington 98101
   (206) 624-5480

A curriculum guide for community trainers responsible for conducting parenting
groups and for getting in touch with parenting.

8. Raising Children's Self-Esteem: A
   Handbook for Parents Association
   for Personal and Organizational
   Development
   APOD Publications
   1427 1st Avenue
   Capitola, California 95010

A wealth of practical advice for managing
children, classrooms, and schools in positive ways. Tapes and books included.

9. Cooperative Extension Office
   3939 Merle Hay Road
   Des Moines, Iowa 50310

Bibliography and several hand outs on
Self-Esteem:
   1. Helping my Child Develop Self-
    . Esteem
   2. My Name is Me
   3. Helping Children Build Self-Esteem
   4. Self-Esteem Indicator

10. Encylopedia Britannica
    Educational Corporation
    425 N. Michigan Avenue
    Chicago, Illinois 60611

Two multimedia resource kits for young
children and parents
   1. Myself and Me
   2. Values: Right or Wrong
These kits consist of five filmstrips with
corresponding tapes and a teacher's guide
with specific educational objectives.

11. Mental Health is 1, 2, 3
    Mental Health Association
    2400 Reading Road
    Cincinnati, Ohio 45202

Practical ideas concerning guidance for
parents as they "Set the Stage" for the
child's life. 100/$1.35

12. What Every Child Needs
    The National Association for Mental
    Health, Inc.
    10 Columbus Circle
    New York, New York 10019

Another practical guide for parents on
child development concepts. $1.00

13. Johnson & Johnson Baby
    Products Co.
    Box 36
    Wicksville, New York 11802

"Maternal Attachment and Mothering
Disorders." A pedictic "round table" publication specific to the needs of parents.
Other materials on communication, learning, and social skills are also available.

14. Consortium, Inc.
    855 Broadway
    Boulder, Colorado 80302

Annotated bibliography on values clarification materials and description of application approaches.

15. Parent Talk — A Regular Feature
    Article
    Sunshine Press
    Scottsdale, Arizona 85201

A series of one-page bulletins suitable
for parents of young children. For example, the bulletin titled "What Kind of
Parent Am I?", Volume 1. #4, is a
questionnaire/rating scale that parents can
self-administer.

16. Super Me, Super You
    Superintendent of Documents
    U.S. Government Printing Office
    Washington, D. C. 20402

A bilingual self-concept activity book
for young children. Comes with a Super
Me guide for parents, teachers, older
brothers and sisters. Contains stories,
drawings, cut outs, games, etc.

17. American Guidance Service
    Publishing Building
    Circle Pines, Minnesota 55014

Catalog of appropriate activity supplies
that new parents would be interested in
purchasing. Catalogue is free of charge.

18. Research Press Films
    Box 31773
    Champaign, Illinois 61820

Films on topics especially suitable for parents, i. e., Parents and Children (proper use of rewards); Behavioral Principles for Parent; and others. Comes with teacher's guide.

19. Professional Educational Department
The National Foundation— March of Dimes
Box 2000
White Plains, New York 10602

A collection of prenatal development materials useful for training.

20. B. L. Winch and Associates
45 Hitching Post Drive, Bldg. 20
Rolling Hills Estates, Ca. 90274

A collection of books for all children as well as many learning materials for normal and gifted. Catalogue free.

21. National Dairy Council
6500 Rosewood
Chicago, Illinois 60606
(312) 696-1020

Check for local or area office and write for a listing of useful materials, i. e., Food Before Six.

22. Enjoy Your Child
Public Affairs Pamphlet #141.
James L. Humes, Jr.
381 Park Avenue, South
New York, New York 10016

A variety of pamphlets appropriate for parents.

23. Family Life Education Curriculum Guide/$16
Vocational Educational and Home Economics Adult Education
Instructional Materials Lab
The Ohio State University
1885 Neil Avenue
Columbus, Ohio 43210

Curriculum guide for teachers containing various units including home care, nutrition, and nursery school planning and implementation. The units include overall goals, concepts, activities, and handout forms. The guide is updated and an excellent resource for any teacher or prospective parent educator.

24. Warren Publishing House,
"The Totline"
Activity Newsletter
P. O. Box 2253
Alderwood Manor, WA 98036

A newsletter published six times a year for people with children, it has a wealth of ideas that are easy to read and understand. $5.00

25. Education for Parenthood
Curriculum Guide
U. S. Department of H. E. W.
Office of Human
Development Services
Admin. of Children, Youth,
and Families,
Children Bureau
Washington DC 20402

Publication # (OHDS) 77-30125. A guide prepared to assist school agencies and community-based organizations in developing parenthood programs.

26. The Decision to Parent
A Teaching Guide
The Iowa State University Press
Ames, IA 50010

An organized set of competency modules planned to assist individuals in: 1. making decisions regarding the assumption of parental responsibilities, and 2. appreciating the factors involved and the skills needed to be an effective parent.

27. John F. Kennedy Center for
Research in Education and Human
Development
George Peabody College for
Teachers
Nashville, TN 37203

Home Visiting with Mothers and Infants. A procedural manual on implementing approaches and processes for a Home Visiting Program. Includes observations and evaluations.

28. Parenting
Parent's Workbook
American Red Cross (check local phone book for nearest office)

29. Appalachia Educational Laboratory
    1031 Wuarrier Street
    P. O. Box 1348
    Charleston, WV 25325

An extensive annotated catalogue of parenting materials on a wide range of appropriate topics.

30. Workshop Models for Family Life
    Education
    Parent-Child Communication
    Family Srvice Association
    of America
    44 East 23rd Street
    New York, New York 10010

A series of manuals exploring new alternatives and the utilization of new options in day-to-day living family life education. Contains training content information, handouts, and practice exercises.

31. Parent Education Newsletter/
    Directory
    Family Health Association, Inc.
    3300 Chester Avenue
    Cleveland, Ohio 44114

A newsletter containing information on numerous resources and parenting topics.

32. The Single Parent
    Journal of Parents Without Partners
    7910 Woodmont Avenue
    Washington, DC 20014

Journal for the Parents Without Partners organization. Contains practical hints for child/family activities and for single parent living.

33. Development and Behavior From
    Birth to Five Years
    Bulletin #437
    Cooperative Extension Services
    Michigan State University
    East Lansing, Michigan 48823

A bulletin of concise but easy-to-understand developmental information.

34. Child Guidance Techniques
    Bulletin #521
    Cooperative Extension Service

The Ohio State University
Columbus, Ohio 43215

A practical guide of child management techniques. Easy to read and arranged according to developmental behavior.

35. Fun in the Making
    U. S. Department of H. E. W.
    Superintendent of Ducuments
    U. S. Government Printing Offices
    Washington, DC 20402

Booklet containing ideas for parents who make children's toys and games. They are simple and fun to make and they encourage chidren to learn and practice specific basic skills. The toys can be made from throw away materials. October, 1979 #(OHDS) 74-031.

36. Your Child and Reading — How
    You Can Help
    Primer for Parents
    Houghton and Mifflin
    1900 South Batavia Avenue
    Geneva, IL 60134

An inexpensive packet giving suggestions for parents in assisting the child to learn to read.

37. R's and A Big Hug
    The Economics Press, Inc.
    12 Daniel Road
    Fairfield, NJ 07006

An inexpensive packet to help parents understand the education process.

38. PTA — Give Your Child A Good
    Start
    National Congress of Parents and
    Teachers
    700 N. Rush Street
    Chicago, IL 60611

An inexpensive pamphlet for parents and for integration into education and children workshops. 35 for $1.00

39. A-B-C's of a Parent Teacher
    Conference
    Your Child's Potential to Learn

Channing L. Bette Company, Inc.
Greenfield, MA 01301

Two bulletins for parent discussion groups
or for general distribution. 25¢

40. Reading Begins At Home
World Book Encyclopedia — Field
Enterprises Education Corp.
Merchandise Mart Plaza
Chicago, IL 60654

An inexpensive bulletin for distribution
to parents. 5¢

41. Let's Find Out
Scholastic Magazine
50 West 44th Street
New York, NY 01136

Beautifully designed ideas for parents
interested in teaching their own children.

42. Activities for Infant Education
John F. Kennedy Child
Development Center
University of Colorado
Medical Center
Denver, CO 80220

A collection of language, personal-social,
fine and gross motor activities. Also includes rhymes and games, suggestions
for home made toys, evaluation of com-
mercial toys, and the importance of music
for babies and toddlers.

43. Cooperative Extension Services
I.S.U. of Science and Technology
Ames, IA 50010

What'a a Parent to Do? Excellent for
parent training relative to planning activities for children.

44. Cooperative Extension Service,
Campbell Hall
Ohio State University
Columbus, OH 43210

A variety of handout or training materials, i.e., PEP (Practical Education for
Parenting); Little people explore the world
of food, etc.

45. The Home Start Demonstration
Program: An Overview
U.S. Department of H.E.W.
Office of Human Development,
OCD
Box 1182
Washington, DC 20013

A publication to acquaint students with
the overall Home Start Program and its
evaluation plan, as well as, provide an
introduction to the sixteen individual
programs throughout the country.

46. Effective Parenting
American Guidance Service
Publishers Bldg.
Circle Pines, MN 55014

A newsletter for sponsors of parent training. Particularly designed to STEP
(Systematic Training for Effective Parenting).

47. National Office, Parents Anonymous
22330 Hawthorne Blvd. , Suite 208
Torrance, CA 90505

A variety of publications appropriate for
distribution and training.

48. Midwest Parent-Child Review
The University of Wisconsin-
Milwaukee
School of Social Welfare
Center for Advanced Studies in
Human Development
P.O. Box 786
Milwaukee, WI 53201

A newsletter which reviews programs and
gives information related to child abuse.

49. Region V.C.A.N. Resource Center
UWM School of Social Welfare
Box 786
Milwaukee, WI 53201

An information Packet (#2) for volunteers on Child Abuse and Neglect programs.

50. Institute for Educational
Development
999 North Sepulveda Blvd.

El Segundo, CA 90245

A report on volunteers, volunteer training materials and a volunteer's guide.

51. You Can Improve Your Child's
    School
    National Committee of Citizens In
    Education
    Suite 410-B Wilde Lake Village
    Green
    Columbia, MD 21044

Answers to more than 200 questions pertaining to parent education and community support systems.

52. Citizen Participation
    Rapids Press
    1460 Koll Circle
    San Jose, CA 95112

An extensive compilation of programs on citizen participation. Also includes points on evaluation and implementation.

53. Parents Anonymous National Office
    2810 Artesia Boulevard
    Redondo Beach, CA 90278

Resource materials for parent education groups concerned with child abuse. Toll free #: 800-421-0353

54. Ohio Department of Public Welfare
    Children' Protective Services
    30 East Broad Streeet, 30th Floor
    Columbus, OH 43215

A prevention and reporting kit that contains a variety of condensed materials suitable for teaching parents and/or students.

55. *National Analysis of Official Child
    Neglect and Abuse Reporting*
    American Humane Association
    5351 S. Roslyn St.
    Englewood, CA 80110

Full analysis of the official reports of child neglect and abuse as submitted by participating states. $6.00

56. American Child Care Services
    32 Settlers Landing Road
    P.O. Box 548
    Hampton, VA 23669 (804) 722-4495

A library of cassette tapes pertinent to children's welfare. In addition, this private foundation maintains bibliographic and child care personnel clearing houses.

57. American Lung Association of
    Michigan
    403 Seymour Avenue
    Lansing, MI 48914

An easy-to-read pamphlet illustrating directions for prevention of choking from small toys, household items, etc. Excellent for use as parent handouts.

58. U.S. Consumer Product Safety
    Commission
    Bureau of Information and Education
    Washington, DC 20207
    Toll Free 800-638-2666

Free and practical guides to safer conditions for parents and children (safety precautions, a guide to reaching poison prevention, etc.). Relevant to parent training.

59. Columbus AAA Club
    174 East Long Street
    Columbus, OH 43215
(Check directory for local listing of American Automobile Assocation).

Terry the Tricycle— small booklets for children on safety and maintenance of their tricycles. Leaflets teach young children to cope with today's residential traffic.

60. Mattel Toys, Mattel, Inc.
    5150 Rosecrans Avenue
    Hawthorne, CA 90250

An excellent toy buying guide for parent training groups. Includes points on safety, suitability, and developmental appropriateness of toys.

61. U.S. Department of H.E.W.
    Office of Human Development

Services
Administration for Children, Youth
and Families
Superintendent of Documents
U.S. Government Printing Office
Washington, DC 20402

A. A Tale of Shots and Drops
(#OHDS 79-31128
B. Can Food Stamps Help You? #1225
C. How to Apply for and Use Food
Stamps #1226
D. Parents guide to Immigration
#OHDS 77-50058
E. A Parent's Guide to Day Care
#OHDS 80-30254
F. The Role of Parents as Teachers
#602-072158
G. A Guide for Parents and Parent
Advisory Councils #1780-1231

62. United Graphics
P.O. Box 24287
Seattle, WA 98124

A booklet of instructions for teaching
small children to use the telephone in an
emergency.

63. Michigan Office of Highway Safety
Planning
7150 Harris Drive
Lansing, MI 48913

Information and educational materials relative to safety and child restraint facts.

64. The Parent Scene
School of Health
Loma Linda University
Loma Linda, CA 92350

Parenting seminars newsletter presents
topics and resources for parents. Published quarterly.

65. A Safe Home for Your Children
Mead Johnson and Co.
Evansville, IN 47721

Booklet which discusses common household hazards, suggests ways to prevent
accidents and actions to take if an accident occurs.

66. Ohio Department of Health
Accident Prevention Unit
Box 118
Columbus, OH 43216

An annotated collection or printed and
audio-visual resources for training.

67. Children's Safety Lessons
Kemper Insurance Co.
Long Grove, IL 60047

An excellent booklet on safety written for
children. May be used as handouts for
parents.

68. Questor Juvenile Furniture Co.
Kantwet Division
771 N. Freedom H. Department.
PML
Ravenna, OH 44266

Guide covers the gamut of how to travel
with babies and toddlers. Free.

69. A Safe World for Babies
and Toddlers
Johnson and Johnson
New Brunswick, NJ 08903

A free booklet suitable for teaching parents about accident prevention.

70. Learning Seed Company
145 Brentwood Drive
Palative, IL 60067

A multimedia kit including two filmstrips
with cassettes, a copy of "Snacks Digest,"
and teaching guide. Discusses how nutri-
tionally inappropriate snacking can be
kept to a minimum.

71. Sesame Street Activities Book
Children's Television Workshop
1 Lincoln Plaza
New York, NY 10023

A collection of activities that can be used
with the child as a follow up to the
Sesame Street TV show.

72. National PTA Office
700 North Rush Street
Chicago, IL 60611

This resource kit offers general information on the need for education for parenthood as part of the curriculum of public schools. Single copies are free.

73. Midwest Parent-Child Review
    The University of Wisconsin-Milwaukee
    School of Social Welfare
    Center for Advanced Studies in Human Development
    P.O. Box 786
    Milwaukee, WI 53201

A newsletter which reviews programs and gives information related to child abuse.

74. Region V.C. A.N. Resource Center
    UWM School of Social Welfare
    Box 786
    Milwaukee, WI 53201

An Information Packet (#2) for volunteers on Child Abuse and Neglect programs.

75. Institute for Educational Development
    999 North Sepulveda Blvd.
    El Segundo, CA 90245

A report on volunteers, volunteer training materials and a volunteer's guide.

76. The Meeting Will Come to Order
    Parliamentary Procedures— Ext.
    Bulletin 294
    Michigan State University
    East Lansing, MI 48823

A bulletin useful for developing parent leadership skills.

77. The Adult Education Association,
    NEA
    Washington, DC

Parenting leadership pamphlets:
#1 How to Lead a Discussion, 1955
#5 How to Teach Adults Leadership, 1955
#6 How to Use Role Playing, 1955

78. Child, Inc.

818 East 53rd Street
Austin, TX 78751

The Manual of Ethics and Procedures. Written by parents for parents to help them in understanding what they can and should do as a policy member. $1.00

79. Citation Press
    A Division of Scholastic
    50 West 44th Street
    New York, NY 10036

A clear concise explanation of the volunteers' job. Offers practical advice on how to capture and keep the child's interest. $2.85.

80. National School Public Relations
    Association
    1201 16th Street, NW
    Washington, DC 20036

Conference Time: For Teachers and Parents. A 1970 teacher's guide to conference reporting. An excellent source with prctical information. $2.00.

81. The Rights of Parents in the Education of Their Children
    National Committee for Citizens in Education
    Columbia, MD 21044

#108 — Useful in developing parent policy groups. By D. Schimmel and L. Fisher. $2.95.

82. Educational Equity Group
    National Institute of Education,
    DHEW
    Washington, DC 20014

Proceedings: Conference on Corporal Punishment in the Schools, A National Debate, School of Social Relations, 1977, free.

83. Home and School Institute
    Trinity College
    Washington, DC 20017

A Family Affair: Education and 101 Activities for Building More Effective School Community Involvement, Publication to assist in building home/school/community partnerships in education.

84. PAR— Department D.C.
    464 Central Avenue
    Northfield, IL 60093

Directions for parents, using everyday objects for enjoyable learning activities for children. $2.50.

85. The National Center for Voluntary Action
    1785 Massachusetts Avenue, NW
    Washington, DC 20036

Volunteers in Child Abuse Prevention Programs and Volunteer Recogniton. A guide and resource for training.

86. Volunteers in Social Justice
    The National Information Center on Volunteerism
    1221 University Avenue
    Boulder, CO 80302

General information on the development and implementation of volunteer programs.

87. Central Texas Council of Governments
    302 East Central
    Bleton, TX 76513

A quarterly newsletter on volunteer programs.

88. The Effective Management of Volunteer Programs.
    Volunteer Management Associates
    279 South Cedar Brook Road
    Boulder, CO 80302

An excellent reference on the how to's and why's, by Marlene Wilson, 1977.

89. How To Organize an Effective Parent Group and Move Bureaucracies
    Coordinating Council for Handicapped Children
    407 South Dearborn
    Chicago, IL 60605

90. A Parents Network
    The National Committee for Citizens in Education
    Suite 410 Wilde Lake Village Green
    Columbia, MD 21044

A fund raising manual for use by parent/citizen groups.

91. The National Committee for Citizens in Education
    Suite 410 Wilde Lake Village Green
    Columbia, MD 21044

Developing leadership for parent/citizen groups, a Parents Network publication.

92. The Committee on Academic Freedom of the American Civil Liberties Union (ACLU)
    22 E. 40th Street
    New York, NY 11016

Working papers are available on request.

93. Accidental Life Insurance Company of California
    Olive at 12th Street
    Los Angeles, CA 90015

Various free pieces of literature related to lay group organizations.

94. Parents Without Partners, Inc.
    P.O. Box 334
    Toledo, OH 43691

A newsletter describing activities, opportunities, and the nature of the organization. May also contact local PWP groups.

95. Family Health Association, Inc.
    3300 Chester Avenue
    Cleveland, OH 44114

Sample newsletter

96. Division of Early Childhood and Special Education
    Office of Instructional Services
    Georgia Department of Education
    Atlanta, GA 30334

"A Parent Guide to PL 94-142" Pamphlet explains the federal law in terms parents can understand.

97. Division for the Blind and Physically Handicapped
    Library of Congress
    Washington, DC 20542

Free talking book service of the Library of Congress for children and adults unable to read regular printed materials.

98. Wardell Associates, Inc.
    49 Pickney Street
    Boston, MA 02114

Educational kits for helping special children learn: 1. Pattern of English; 2. Flying Start Learning to Learn Kit; 3. Flying Start Extension Kit; 4. Learning About numbers.

99. Play Schools Association
    120 W. 57th Street
    New York, NY 10019

Offers a variety of parent training materials.

100. Elementary, Kindergarten, Nursery Education (E.K.N.E.)
     2101 Sixteenth Street, NW
     Washington, DC 20002

This professional organization offers pertinent, inexpensive training materials.

101. The Parenting Materials Information Center
     Early Childhood Division
     Southwest Educational Development Laboratory
     211 E. 7th Street
     Austin, TX 78701

Wide variety of excellent training materials.

102. Moreno Educational Co.
     7050 Belle Glade Lane
     San Diego, CA 92119

Spanish parenting materials.

103. The Center for Family and Child Development
     Three Carhart Avenue
     White Plains, NY 10605

Write directly for list of available resources.

104. Center for the Study of Parent Involvement
     2544 Aetna Street
     Berkeley, CA 94704

Write for a listing of available resources.

105. National Legal Resource Center on Child Advocacy and Protection
     American Bar Association
     1800 M Street, NW, 2nd Floor
     Washington, DC 20036

This agency funds various child advocacy projects.

106. The Profession of Parenting Institute
     1609 Poplar Street
     Philadelphia, PA 19130

Write for a listing of available resources.

107. PARTNERS
     4215 Sunset Drive
     Jackson, MS 39213

Report on Jackson Public Schools Parent Education Demonstration Project.

Films — Multi-media:

1. Parenting Pictures
   121 N.W. Crystal Street
   Crystal River, FL 32629

Caring and Coping: The New Parenting Experience. Designed to introduce the concept of parenting education, normal concerns of parents, and caring methods. For professionals and parents.

2. Parents Magazine Films, Inc.
   Department C
   52 Vanderbilt Avenue
   New York, New York 10017

A wide variety of films and film strip presentations on child development topics. Suitable for parents. Catalogue free.

3. Parenting Materials
   Appalachia Educational Laboratory
   1031 Querrier Street, Box 1348
   Charleston, WV 25325

An annotation of audiovisuals for effective parenting.

4. Sunburst
   Room 3636
   39 Washington Avenue
   Pleasantville, NY 10370

Many color sound filmstrips suitable for parent training programs. Catalog free.

5. Footsteps — A television series on parenting.

Footsteps focuses on some of the problems and concerns that all parents of young children face. Call your local public TV station. Developed by a consortium of Applied Managment Sciences, Silver Springs, MD

6. Action for Children's Television
   46 Austin Street
   Newtonville, MA 02160

Write for a catalogue

7. Terro Films
   Film Library
   31 Roberts Hall, Cornell University
   Ithaca, NY 14850

What's Good to Eat — For Parents and Students
Food, the Color of Life

8. Human Services Development
   Catalog
   1616 Soldiers Field Road
   Boston, MA 02135

Write for catalog

9. National Citizens Committee for
   Broadcasting
   1028 Connecticut Ave., NW
   Washington, DC 20036

This organization will send you names of local citizen media groups in your region. Will also provide other useful materials.

10. Parents Television Guide
    The Quaker Oats Company
    Corporate Affairs Dept.
    Merchandise Mart Plaza
    Chicago, IL 60654

Tips about rewarding ways to watch and discuss television with children.

11. Career Kits for Kids
    Encyclopedia Britannica Educational
    Corporation
    425 N. Michigan Avenue
    Chicago, IL 60611

Multimedia package designed to help a child understand a certain profession. Each kit contains a filmstrip, stencils for games, pages to color, and a teacher's guide listing the concepts involved and explanations of the activities.

12. Jr. League of Louisville
    627 W. Main Street
    Louisville, KY 40202

Whose Child Is This? 16 mm; 30 min., color; Follows a chronological sequence from detection, reporting, investigation, removal of child through pre-trial.

13. Information Officer
    Arkansas MR-DDS
    Suite 400 Walden Bldg.
    7th and Main
    Little Rock, AR 72201

Public Servie Campaign Packet, samples of multi media campaigns. Designed to educate the various publics about mental retardation and developmental disabilities.

14. Supt. is the Heart of the Child —
    Film
    Operation Cork
    P.O. Box 9550
    San Diego, CA 92109

16 mm; 30 min., color; Sensitive, realistic picture of the web of alcoholism — one which entangles the entire family.

15. National Committee of Citizens in
    Education
    Suite 410-B Wilde Lake

Village Green
Columbia, MD 21044

A series of five slide-tape presentations
based on Citizens Training Institutes.
Running time for each film: 12 to 15
minutes. Individual filmstrips may be purchased for $27.50, the full set of five for
$110. Preview for $5.00 per film. (Fee
can be applied to purchase price.)

16. GPN
    Box 80669
    Lincoln, NE 68501

Teaching Infants and Toddlers. Seven
programs ranging from 8½ to 12½
minutes.

17. Child Abuse and Neglect Audio-
    Visual Materials
    The National Center on
    Child Abuse and Neglect
    Box 1182
    Washington, DC 20013

The directory includes 215 items pre-
viewed by the center and includes services for videotapes, films, slides, cassettes, and multimedia packages on child
abuse and neglect.

Humanics Limited • Humanics New Age

INFANT AND TODDLER

Humanics National Infant-Toddler Assessment Handbook
Infant and Toddler Handbook
Toddlers Learn by Doing: Activities for Toddlers & Activity Log
For Parents and Teachers

ACTIVITY BOOKS

Aerospace Projects for Young Children
Art Projects for Young Children
Back to Basics in Reading Made Fun
Birthdays: A Celebration
Children Around the World
Child's Play
Early Childhood Activities
Energy
Exploring Feelings
Fingerplays and Rhymes For Always and Sometimes
Handbook of Learning Activities
Metric Magic
Month By Month Activity Guide
Scissor Sorcery: Cutting Activities For Early Childhood Programs
Vanilla Manila Folder Games

EARLY CHILDHOOD EDUCATION

Alternative Approaches to Educating Young Children
Bloomin' Bulletin Boards
Can Piaget Cook?
Competencies
Feelings
Freedom to Grow
Learning Environments for Children
Leaves Are Falling in Rainbows
Looking At Children
Nuts and Bolts
Planning Outdoor Play
Storybook Classrooms
The Whole Teacher
Young Children's Behavior

CHILD ASSESSMENT

Childrens Adaptive Behavior Report (CABR)
Childrens Adaptive Behavior Scale (CABS)

Humanics Limited • Humanics New Age

CHILD ASSESSMENT

Humanics National Preschool Assessment Handbook
The Lollipop Test

SPECIAL EDUCATION

EARLI Program Vol. I
EARLI Program Vol. II
LATON: The Parent Book
New Approaches to Success in the Classroom

SCHOOL COUNSELING

H. E. L. P. for the Adolescent
Humanics Limited System for Record Keeping
I Live Here Too
Real Talk Student's Manual
Real Talk Teacher's Manual
When I Grow Up Vol. I
When I Grow Up Vol. II

PARENT INVOLVEMENT

Better Meetings
Building Successful Parent-Teacher Partnerships
Dialog for Parents
Emotionally Yours
Family Enrichment Trainee's Manual
Family Enrichment Trainer's Manual
Handbook for Involving Parents In Education
Handbook of Reading Activities
Lives of Families
Love Notes
Parents and Beginning Reading
Parents and Teachers
Reading Roots
Working Together

HUMANICS NEW AGE BOOKS

The Best Chance Diet
Body Conditioning
Body, Spirit, and Soul
Kids Who Hate School
The Love Book For Couples
Midlife Myths and Realities
The Tao of Leadership

More Parent Involvement Books
From Humanics Limited

Building Successful Parent/Teacher Partnerships
R. Eleanor Duff, Ph. D., Carol F. Hobson, Ph. D.,
Kevin Swick, Ph. D.

Building Successful Parent/Teacher Partnerships provides the authoritative solutions to problems that have led many parents and teachers to become disenchanted with parent involvement programs. This text examines the changing nature of parenting and teaching in recent decades, and gives you a comprehensive, workable plan for implementing a successful parent/teacher involvement program, in *any* educational setting. $ 9.95

Working Together:
A Guide to Parent Involvement
Anthony J. Coletta, Ph. D.

All of us recognize the need to establish or renew a sense of trust between the home and school. Parent/teacher partnerships should be based on clear *communication* and *reciprocity. Working Together* envisions just that: parents and teachers *working together* toward helping children meet their needs for survival, growth and happiness. This thoughtful manual includes plans for parent participation in the classroom, alternative approaches to teaching parenting skills, suggested home based activities, supplements to parent programs and helpful child development guides and checklists. $14.95

Handbook Of Reading Activities
From Teacher To Parent To Child
Mac Henry Brown, Carl F. Brown

Help Parents Help! Finally you have a convenient, easy-to-use program which gives you just what you need to establish a home/school partnership for teaching children basic reading skills! Use *Handbook of Reading Activities* to take advantage of a child's first and most important learning resource— his parents. *Handbook of Reading Activities* contains activities in the areas of visual discrimination, auditory discrimination, learning letter names and phonics, suitable for both developmental and remedial reading programs. Simply send appropriate activities home with the parent and child for individual practice and attention at home! With *Handbook of Reading Activities* students who need a little extra help to master basic reading skills can get that help at *home*. Parents will enjoy being an active participant in their child's learning process. And all of you— teacher, parent and child— will experience together the joy and satisfaction that comes from learning. $12.95

Parents and Beginning Reading
Mary Jett-Simpson, Ph. D.

Parents are the single most powerful influence on children's development— and no one is in a better position to instill a love of reading in children. This highly readable text tells parents how. It includes an overview of children's language development, suggestions for games that enhance reading skills, ideas for establishing a reading environment in the home, lists of resources, and a thorough evaluation of the many kinds of books available for young readers. $14.95

Order these books or request a catalog of Humanics Limited's full line of books for educators and parents from:
Humanics Limited, P.O. Box 7447, Atlanta, Georgia 30309
(404) 874-2176
Collect calls for Mastercard or Visa orders are accepted.